The
Muslim
Student's
Guide

to University and Beyond

Idris Zahoor

Ta-Ha Publishers Ltd.

© 1432 AH/2011 CE Ta-Ha Publishers Ltd.
Shaban 1432 AH/July 2011 CE

Ta-Ha Publishers Ltd,
Unit 4, The Windsor Centre,
Windsor Grove, West Norwood,
London, SE27 9NT
UK

Website: www.taha.co.uk
E-mail: sales@taha.co.uk

Written by: Idris Zahoor
General Editor: Dr. Abia Afsar-Siddiqui
Book and Cover Design by: Shakir Abdulcadir » www.opensquares.co.uk

A catalogue record of this book is available from the British Library
ISBN-13: 978-1-84200-126-4

Printed and bound by: IMAK Ofset, Turkey

We acknowledge the following bodies for the images in this book:
Page 6: http://en.wikipedia.org/wiki/File:Chinese_fonts_juhuasample.PNG
Page 9: View of Africa and Saudi Arabia from Apollo 17 taken on 7th December 1972 by the Apollo 17 astronauts. Thanks to NASA and the NSSDC (http://nssdc.gsfc.nasa.gov).
Pages 9, 10, 11: http://www.rense.com/general72/size.htm

Dedication

I would like to dedicate this book to my mother and father, for whom I do not have the words to express my gratitude for all their love, support and privileged upbringing they have provided me. To my big brother who has always been just that to me and always looked out for me... To my late sister whose soul I hope is smiling away in the heavens and last but not least, to my wife who continues to encourage me in everything I do and without whom I'd be lost.

Contents

Introduction

I begin in the name of Allah, the Most Beneficent, the Most Merciful.

Allah mentions several times in the Qur'an that the successful ones are those that think deeply, contemplate and look around them at His creation for evidence and signs that all point to the Creator Himself.

I once heard someone say that 'life was like a test', which made me think. The first thing I thought of was all the academic tests that I had sat in school. The more I thought about it, the more I could see the similarities between my time spent at university and the life of this world. That was the starting point for writing this book.

The aim of this book is mainly to guide you and help you make an informed and proactive start to your university life so that you can get the best out of your short time here. It also highlights the similarities between university life and life in general. For me, the comparison seemed to make the process and purpose of life easier to understand. I hope that it will do the same for you as well and, *insha'Allah*, make it easier to do well in both.

Throughout the book, I have drawn from the Qur'an and authentic *Hadith*, without which no book on Islam would be complete. In addition I have used inspirational quotes from some great Islamic scholars which I felt were relevant to the topic in question.

A book of this nature touches upon many different Islamic concepts, ideas and rulings rather than focusing on just one topic and so it has not been possible to discuss each topic in any great detail. There are many books written by great scholars on all aspects of our lives that are relevant to us today. My intention is to ignite the spark of curiosity here and I would urge you to follow up with your own further reading if you wish to study a particular subject in depth, with the bibliography at the end as a possible starting point.

Regardless of whether we have a little knowledge or a great deal, Islam makes it obligatory for us to communicate it to others. May Allah accept my feeble effort to gain His pleasure and His pleasure alone. Ameen.

Last but not least, I wish you every success during your time at university and beyond.

Idris Zahoor

Chapter 1

What is the Point?

Who? Where? Why? What Next?

Congratulations! You have left school and are about to start on the final leg of your formal academic education. You will no doubt have been given lots of advice and opinions about university life, but above all, many people will tell you to make the most of your time here. And there is a good reason for that.

Universities are almost like a little world of their own. From professors that are internationally renowned specialists in their field, to researchers searching for new discoveries through to students who are keen to gain knowledge, everybody is here to make a difference with information, knowledge and ideas that benefit the individual, society and the economy.

Rather than just being a bigger version of school, university is a place where you are encouraged to think and act for yourself. What you get out of university depends very much on the choices that you make and how much effort you are prepared to put in. There isn't an attendance register or anyone telling you what you should do. But if you choose to attend the extra tutorials, do the recommended reading, find out about your department's next networking event then you will reap the dividends. The opportunities will not come to you, you have to go out and seek them.

So why are you actually at university (apart from the fact that your parents want you to!)? Perhaps it is because you stand a better chance of getting a good job; to become an expert in a certain profession of interest; or simply to be in a profession with a good salary. Well that was the case with me, anyway. I wanted to become a building surveyor because it was a well-paid profession.

Whether you have enrolled purely for financial gain, self-enlightenment or any other reason, you will have done so with a purpose in mind and hence your time at university becomes a means to an end goal. You are there for a period of time, you make the most of it according to what you want and then move onto the next stage in your life.

Apart from a very small number of students who fall in love with the university lifestyle and extend their stay for as long as possible, the majority of students nearing the end of their course realise the temporary nature of university life, the need to move on and to prepare for the next stage in their careers.

So bearing in mind that our life on earth is also temporary, the only way we can get the best out of it is to work out what our goal is. What is the purpose of life? Why are we here? How did we get here? Where are we going to go?

Imagine this scenario: you are going about your daily routine when you are kidnapped, blindfolded and taken to an unknown place. Several thoughts and questions are going through your head at this point but there are probably four key questions that stand out.

» Firstly, you want to know WHO has had the audacity to do this to you;

» Secondly, you want to know WHERE you are;

» Thirdly, you are probably wondering WHY this is happening to you;

» Finally, you are dreading the thought of WHAT will happen to you NEXT.

In a way, every one of us is in this predicament and we need to know the answers. We need to know WHO has put mankind on earth, what is the reality of WHERE we are, WHY we are here and WHAT will happen NEXT when we die. Yes, that's right, die! It might sound morbid to talk about death but it is inevitable so we are going to have to face it sooner or later.

Now these are seriously deep questions. No doubt the greatest minds from among mankind have been pondering about these since the start of the human race and come up with all sorts of complex theories from different philosophical, scientific and theological points of view. So how can we ordinary people even begin to look for the answers to these questions?

The Limited Nature of Man

We need to remember that Man by his very nature is limited in every sense. We live a finite life, we can only see up to a certain point, we can only hear at limited volumes and within given distances and so on. Our minds can only comprehend something, say an object, if we have seen someone use that object or if we are given certain previous information by somebody else about the object.

Take, for example, reading Chinese. If you have never been taught Chinese, never heard it or never seen it in written format and you were given a page of Chinese literature to read, would you be able to read it? Would you be able to read it if you tried hard enough without anybody's help or any other information? Give it a try and see if you can read this. Take your time...

你的黃花滿地傷

你的黃花滿地傷

你的黃花滿地傷

的黃華滿地傷

的黃華滿坤傷

Any luck? Try for as long as you like but you will not be able to unless somebody who knows Chinese reads out the writing whilst you listen and repeat or you are taught how the language is written.

If we can't even work out something as small as this unless someone tells us what it is, how can we possibly comprehend the Creator of the universe and all that exists within and beyond it? The answer is we can't. Not unless we are given some authentic information from the Creator Himself or through His Messengers.

To put it another way: when we buy any product, be it an electrical appliance or a car, it comes with an operating manual produced by the manufacturer of the product. The manual tells us how to make the best and most effective use of the item and also gives us warnings of the things to avoid which will be detrimental to the product or to our own health, such as 'keep away from direct sunlight' or 'keep out of reach of children'. When we run into any difficulties with the product, we first turn to the instruction manual and when we need further help, we contact the manufacturer.

Allah, in His infinite kindness and wisdom, has given us a complete and detailed 'manual' in the form of the Qur'an, written by the 'Manufacturer' Himself. So why is it that we accept Allah as our Creator and hence our 'Manufacturer' and yet we ignore the 'Manual' He has given us with its priceless advice and numerous warnings?

The Qur'an gives us all the information that we need to answer our questions, so without further ado, we shall begin by looking at WHERE we are, WHO created us and WHY.

The Creation of the Universe

Science is continually developing theories about how the universe came into being but because of the limited nature of man that we have discussed, we can never truly understand matters beyond our comprehension. Allah has described in great detail in the Qur'an how He created the universe and how life on earth developed.

At the beginning of time, we learn that the universe was one mass that separated out into heavens and earth:

> *Do not the unbelievers see that the heavens and the earth were joined together (as one unit of creation), before we clove them asunder?* (Surah Al-Anbiya' 21:30)

On the earth, all living creatures were made from water:

> *We made from water every living thing.* (Surah Al-Anbiya' 21:30)

The earth was given features such as mountains and pathways:

> *And We have set on the earth mountains standing firm, lest it should shake with them, and We have made therein broad highways (between mountains) for them to pass through that they may receive guidance.* (Surah Al-Anbiya' 21:31)

The sky was initially a dust-like state. Allah then divided the heavens into seven parts, formed celestial bodies such as moons, stars and planets and established night and day:

> *Moreover, He comprehended in His design the sky, and it had been (as) smoke... So He completed them as seven firmaments in two days and He assigned to each heaven its duty and command. And We adorned the lower heaven with lights, and (provided it) with guard...* (Surah Fussilat 41:11-12)

> *And He it is Who created the night and the day, and the sun and the moon. They float, each in an orbit.* (Surah Al-Anbiya' 21:33)

We are not told in the Qur'an what order all this happened in, but we do know that the creation of the universe occurred in six distinct stages or epochs:

> *Your Guardian-Lord is Allah, Who created the heavens and the earth in six days, then He established Himself on the Throne (of authority)...* (Surah Al-A'raf 7:54)

The Size of the Universe

As we have mentioned before, Man's thinking is rather limited and we go about our daily lives with pride and arrogance. We think that we know a great deal about the universe because we've put a man on the moon or sent out unmanned spacecraft into outer space. But the reality is that we cannot even imagine how vast the universe is. 'Ali ibn Abi Talib ﷺ told us of a way to deal with this by saying:

> *Put aside your pride, set down your arrogance and remember your grave.* ('Ali ibn Abi Talib ﷺ)

But let us try (and I emphasise the word 'try' here as our limited nature cannot comprehend these matters!) for a moment to begin to understand the sheer vastness of the universe and how we fit into it based on what we do know.

Imagine yourself standing or sitting wherever you are at the moment. Now zoom out and imagine yourself looking down at planet Earth from outer space.

nssdc.gsfc.nasa.gov

What is the Point?

Have a look at this scale model of the inner planets of our solar system (and Pluto) and you will see that Earth looks big in comparison to Venus, Mars, Mercury and Pluto.

Earth   Venus

Mars   Mercury   Pluto

Keep imagining yourself on Earth as we zoom out further and further until we come up against the bigger outer planets of the Solar System: Jupiter, Saturn, Neptune and Uranus. All of a sudden, planet Earth doesn't seem so large.

The journey continues out to the Sun. Although the Sun may look like a small bright disc in the sky when we look at it from Earth, the picture below shows the true scale of Earth and the other planets against the Sun.

Our sun, which dwarfs all of the planets in the Solar System, is just a baby in comparison to other stars such as Sirius, Pollux and Arcturus.

But in reality, these are not even the biggest stars. Compared to the Supergiant Star, Antares, the Sun is hardly visible and is in fact 800 times smaller.

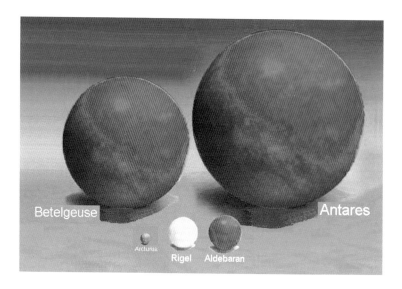

These are just a few of the billions and billions of stars in what we call the universe, but which is actually the lowest of the seven heavens that Allah has created. Al-'Abbas ﷺ reported that the Messenger of Allah ﷺ said:

> *"Do you know what is the distance between the heaven and the earth?" We said: "Allah and His Messenger know best." He ﷺ said: "The distance between them is five hundred years and the distance between one heaven and the next is five hundred years and the dimension of each heaven would take five hundred years to travel and there is a sea between the seventh heaven and the 'Arsh (the Throne of Allah) which has between its lowest and highest ends the distance equivalent to that between the heavens and the earth. And Allah, Most High, is above that and nothing is withheld from Him of the deeds of the sons of Adam."* (Abu Dawud)

Or to put it another way: Abu Dhar ﷺ reported that the Messenger of Allah ﷺ said:

> *"The seven heavens and the seven earths by the side of Al-Kursi (the Footstool of Allah) are naught but as a ring thrown down in a desert land, and such is Al-Kursi with respect to Al-'Arsh (the Throne of Allah)."* (Al-Bayhaqi)

You might like a moment to let that sink in!

Now let's zoom all the way back from Allah's Throne (*Al-'Arsh*) to his Footstool (*Al-Kursi*), back to the supergiant stars, the Sun, the bigger planets, Earth and all the way back to you. How important do you feel now?! We are so insignificant in the great, vast scheme of Allah's creation that we cannot even comprehend it, let alone the Creator of it all Himself:

> *No vision can grasp Him. But His grasp is over all vision. He is above all comprehension, yet is acquainted with all things.*
> (Surah Al-Anam 6:103)

The Creation of Man

Once Allah had created the heavens and the earth and filled them, he made Man:

Your Lord said to the angels, "I am going to create a human being out of clay." (Surah Sad 38:71)

...And then We said to the angels, "Prostrate before Adam," and they prostrated – except for Iblis. He was not among those who prostrated. (Surah Al-A'raf 7:11)

We will come back later to who Iblis was and the exchange that he had with Allah at this point.

Now Adam ﷺ and his wife lived in *Jannah*. She is not mentioned by name in the Qur'an but we know from *hadith* that her name is Hawwa.

"Adam, live in the Garden, you and your wife, and eat of it wherever you like. But do not go near this tree lest you become wrongdoers."

Then Shaytan whispered to them, disclosing to them their private parts that had been concealed from them. He said: "Your Lord has only forbidden you this tree lest you become angels or among those who live for ever."

He swore to them, "I am one of those who give you good advice."

So he enticed then to do it by means of trickery. Then when they tasted the tree, their private parts were disclosed to them and they started stitching together the leaves of the Garden in order to cover themselves. Their Lord called out to them, "Did I not forbid you this tree and say to you, 'Shaytan is an outright enemy to you'?"

They said, "Our Lord! We have wronged ourselves. If you do not forgive us and have mercy on us, we will be among the lost."

He said, "Go down from here as enemies to each other! You will have residence on the earth and enjoyment for a time."

He said, "On it you will live and on it die, and from it you will be brought forth." (Surah Al-'Araf 7:19-25)

This is a very important story and there are many lessons we can learn from it, but mainly that:

» Allah gave Adam ؑ and his wife a multitude of blessings but in return, asked them to stay away from one thing.

» *Shaytan* did not directly tell Adam and Hawwa (peace be upon them) to disobey Allah, but whispered suggestions to them and presented himself to them as their friend and sincere advisor.

» Adam and Hawwa (peace be upon them) had the freedom to choose between good and evil but succumbed to *Shaytan*'s suggestions and so they had to face the consequences of their disobedience to Allah and were sent down to Earth.

» When they realised they had done wrong, they turned to Allah in repentance and Allah forgave them and guided them.

Our lives here on earth, as the descendants of Adam and Hawwa (peace be upon them), mirror that exact situation. We are also blessed with numerous things to enjoy in this world and the promise of Eternal Bliss in the Hereafter, but Allah asks us to keep away from certain things if we wish to attain that state. *Shaytan*, meanwhile, is doing his best to whisper suggestions to make us overstep the bounds of Allah.

But who is *Shaytan* and why is he going to so much trouble to lead us astray?

Allah vs. Shaytan

Shaytan is a creature from the world of *Jinn*. He has many names and is also known as Iblis, Satan and The Devil. *Jinn* are a creation of Allah made from smokeless fire and they are invisible to humans. They are separate and different from both the angels and mankind; however, like mankind, they possess the power of reason and can choose between good and evil. *Jinn* existed before the creation of Adam 🙏.

We left the story of the creation of Adam 🙏 at the point where Iblis refused to obey Allah's command to bow down to this new creation made of clay. What happened next?

He [Allah] said, "What prevented you from prostrating when I commanded you to?" He [Iblis] replied, "I am better than him. You created me from fire and You created him from clay."

He said, "Descend from Heaven. It is not for you to be arrogant in it. So get out! You are one of the abased."

He said, "Grant me a reprieve until the day they are raised up."

He said, "You are one of the reprieved."

He said, "Because of your misguidance of me, I will lie in ambush for them on your straight path. Then I will come at them, from in front of them, from behind them, from their right and from their left. You will not find most of them thankful."

He said, "Get out of it, reviled and driven out. As for those of them who follow you, I will fill up Hell with every one of you." (Surah Al-'Araf 7:12-18)

Shaytan was arrogant, jealous and rebellious. He challenged Allah to let him go free to mislead us into disobeying Allah using every tactic he knew. Allah accepted his request and that is why we find ourselves in the situation we are in today. The challenge continues and will continue until the end of time.

The Freedom to Choose

OK, so what hope have we got of staying on the right path if *Shaytan* and his army are determined to see us fail?

Well that's the beauty of it. Even *Shaytan* knows that the believing Muslim is no match for him and his army and all their whisperings:

> He [Iblis] said, "My Lord, because You misled me, I will make things on the earth seem good to them and I will mislead them all, every one of them, except Your slaves among them who are sincere. Thou hast put me in the wrong, I will make (wrong) fair-seeming to them on the Earth, and I will put them all in the wrong – except Thy servants among them, sincere and purified (by Thy Grace)."
>
> He [Allah] said, "This is a Straight Path to Me. You have no authority over any of My slaves except for the misled who follow you." (Surah Al-Hijr 15:39-42)

We have free will, the freedom to choose between good and evil. If we choose good, then we have the capacity to be better than the angels, but if we choose evil then we have joined *Shaytan*'s army. But it is not an equal contest between good and evil. The scales are loaded in favour of the good, believe it or not. It is imbedded in our nature to recognise Allah and to worship Him.

> I have only created jinns and men, that they may serve Me.
> (Surah Ad-Dhariyat 51:56)

In other words, it is basically easier to be good if we are in tune with our natural human instincts. Allah promises great rewards for all those of His believing servants that follow His path, He knows that we will fail along the way and so in His infinite mercy, He forgives us when we turn to Him in sincere repentance, time after time. And yet most of us are not grateful.

What Next?

And so we come full circle. We started our story of the creation of Man in the Garden and that is where we aim to end up after we die. That is our end goal and this life is just a means to that end goal, just as university is a means to an end goal.

Chapter 2

The Early Days

Of course you are going to be nervous about your first day at university and probably even the first week as you are finding your way around, meeting new people and feeling bewildered by all the opportunities that are available. I don't mind telling you that I was very anxious. But equally, don't let this spoil what is possibly the most exciting time of your university life. And remember that everyone is in exactly the same situation as you.

Before the start of term, you should have received plenty of correspondence from the university. Some of it will be about the various procedures that you need to go through, including course registration, Union membership and ID cards. They may also send you more general information about university facilities, your department, maps of the campus and so on. If you make the time to familiarise yourself with all this as well as browsing the university website, then you will feel more confident and prepared for these first days.

Fresher's Week

The first week of the academic year at university is usually referred to as Freshers' week where a variety of events are held to help and welcome new students. There are a wide range of social activities, including live music and other performance events, sports challenges, stunts and open-air markets especially designed to allow Freshers to make new friends and to get to know others doing the same course. As well as providing a chance to learn about the university, Freshers' week allows you to get to know the city or town which is home to the university and to become familiar with the representatives of your Student Union.

You will also come across a Freshers' Fair for student clubs and societies which is a great way for you to get an idea of the array of facilities on offer, typically outside your course of study. The various societies and clubs available within the university will have stalls and lots of goodies to entice you to join up. These range from sports societies, religious societies, societies for different countries, media societies, community work, politics – you name it and there is probably a society for it. Joining a few gives you the chance to meet like-minded people who share an interest, learn or keep up a skill or just to take a break from all that study!

Do avail yourself of these fantastic opportunities as you will probably not have such a choice again. One of the regrets I have is not signing up for a martial arts course as it was something I always wanted to do but because none of my friends wanted to do it, I left it. On the other hand, you are at university to study so do be careful of not taking on too much and signing up for everything that appeals to you at once. Societies will always welcome you at any time of the year if you decide to join later.

A Small Fish in a Big Pond

Up until now when you were in sixth form or college, you were probably one of a few hundred students on a school site, in other words a big fish in a small pond. Now you will find yourself in a place with tens of thousands of other people on a campus that may be spread all over the city or town. You may be away from home for the first time. The thought of being lonely and without the family and support network you've enjoyed so far may scare you. You might be afraid of not fitting in and so you follow what the crowd is doing. On the other hand, maybe you can't wait to get away from home and all the rules that you feel your parents place on you and cannot wait to sample all the joys that 'freedom' has to offer.

My cousins and brother had told me stories of their university exploits and like most youngsters I looked up (and still do) to my older brother and cousins and could not wait to follow in their footsteps. I will be perfectly honest and say that when I was about to start at university, I was looking forward to being away from the restrictions at home, the night life and so on. But in the summer before I was due to start my university adventures, things changed drastically, or rather my brother and cousins did...

A tragic incident with one of their friends made them change their entire perspective on life. Regular trips to the nightclub became visits to the *masjid*. The immaculate daily clean shaves and aftershave were replaced with beards and *attar*. Qur'an recitations replaced music CDs and evenings were spent studying Islamic history rather than watching movies. Instead of sleeping off the excesses of the previous night's party in the early hours of the morning, they were performing their *Fajr salah*.

The change was so drastic that we all thought they had been brain washed or were involved in some sort of cult. With time though and after many a heated debate, we realised that they had not been brain washed, but because the rest of us had strayed so far from the teachings of Islam, their actions seemed strange to us. Why would anyone choose to do what they did when they could be having a good time?!

Freedom

It then occurred to me that my attitude towards my brother's and cousins' change was so negative because of what I perceived to be the norm.

I recently came across an article in The Times which I have quoted from below as I feel it typifies many people's attitudes to university life and especially the first year.

> *"If there is one thing that has no place at the beginning of university life it is nobility. This is the most permissive moment of your life - a time when, incredibly, you are granted all the freedoms of being a responsible citizen while not being bearing responsibility for so much as buying your own bogroll. Behaviour that would at any other time of life be inexcusably gauche is now not only acceptable, but laudable."[1]*

The reality is that people follow the norms of the society which they have grown up in and are around. It is generally accepted that university is the best time to enjoy 'freedom', in other words to drink, to party and to have relationships and so naturally most people want to experience this to the max.

A Bit of History and Politics

You are probably wondering why I seem to have veered off course and whether either history or politics has any relevance in your life right now. Well bear with me.

If we want to understand people, then we have to learn how and what they think and why they do the things that they do. What you will find is that people's actions reflect what perception they have of life.

---

1 Jack Malvern, Times Online From The Times, August 13 2008

Throughout Western European history, both the State and the Church played a role in determining the daily life of the people. It was always a difficult relationship with one institution wanting greater power than the other. But usually, it was the ruler of the State who was God's representative on Earth and enforced religious and political rule.

However, by the sixteenth century, there were a number of Christian sects and so the Church was not a united body. At the same time, Kings and Emperors were using their 'Divine Right' to exploit and oppress people in the name of religion. This led some philosophers, such as Voltaire, to criticise the place of religion in daily life, arguing that it was intolerant and led to violence.

These thinkers of the so-called 'Age of Reason' or Enlightenment called for a separation of religion and State arguing that Man could understand and gain knowledge of the world around him through reason alone based on scientific evidence. They said that for humans to be good and happy, they should not be restricted by unnecessary religious constraints. Science was the new religion and there was no room for blind faith.

Now when religion plays no part in daily life then Man has to make up rules and laws of his own and follow these. We discussed how Man is very limited in his thinking and so it is like saying that someone should throw away the manufacturer's manual and write one of his own without knowing much about the product!

Of course, when Man is free to make up his own laws then these will be laws based on ideas that suit him: such as the concept of 'freedom', of self-gratification and enjoyment. There is no accountability to anyone so no-one cares about the consequences of these actions. The main point is to enjoy one's self to the full.

Allah tells us in the Qur'an that:

Have you seen him who has taken his whims and desires to be his god? Will you then be his guardian? (Surah Al-Furqan 25:43)

So that's where the society around us is coming from.

Now contrast that with your own situation as a Muslim. You must submit to the will of Allah because that is what the word 'Muslim' means. As Muslims, we have been given a code of life to follow (the Manufacturer's manual that we talked about in the first chapter) and we are accountable to Allah for each and every action that we do, so we need to consider the consequences of our actions. Not only that, but as Muslims in a minority situation, we are also ambassadors for Islam. Most non-Muslims will never read the Qur'an or *hadith* or about Islam. What they know of Islam will come from the Muslims that they meet. YOU can be the reason that someone holds the opinions that they do about Islam.

Back to Freedom Again

There is a *hadith* where Abu Huraira ﷺ reported that the Prophet Muhammad ﷺ said:

> *"The world is a prison for a believer and Paradise for a non-believer."* (Muslim)

Just these few words sum up the whole situation and it is a very powerful *hadith*. In my case, it was life changing. So what did the Prophet ﷺ mean when he said this world is a prison for a believer and Paradise for the non-believer? Well, a believer should be ever mindful of Allah and so he is not free to do as he pleases but must submit to the will of Allah. In this world, we are not free to give in to our desires of eating and drinking whatever we want, giving into our desires of having relationships with whomever we want and satisfying our own whims. We must endure restrictions, trials, suffering and sacrifice in this world in return for a world in which there are none of these things. That is why this world should feel like a prison for a believer.

In contrast to the view that university is the time to enjoy yourself and be free of responsibility, in Islam, people are considered adults once they reach puberty with all the rights and responsibility that

that entails. This can be very confusing for young Muslims because all of their teenage friends of other faiths are not yet considered adults and, therefore, don't seem to have that level of responsibility.

Anyway, the time came when I started university. I had spent the summer in the company of my newly practising brother and cousins and I was reading Islamic books and particularly the commentary to the above *hadith*. With my university being located in Central London, I got to see a whole variety of individuals from all over the UK as well as from abroad; all with different backgrounds and beliefs and overall it was a fantastic eye-opening experience.

However, I could see this *hadith* being borne out in front of my very own eyes straightaway. To a certain extent I still yearned for that freedom and opportunity to 'enjoy' myself but at the same time I would hear the *hadith* reverberate in the back of my mind. I'm not for a second claiming that I became an angel that summer. If anything, a little knowledge had put me in no man's land. I was neither partying the way I had planned to and nor was I fulfilling all my religious duties the way I should have been.

Alcohol

Now coming back to Freshers' Week. I clearly remember my first day at university and the Freshers' week when I was offered 'a pint' by none other than a couple of Muslim brothers who at the time saw no harm in drinking. I am glad to say that Allah had given me enough understanding and courage to be able to say 'no' to their offer. In fact during the course, I became very good friends with the brothers and, *alhamdulillah*, by the end of the course they had stopped drinking alcohol.

Somehow it seems that it is impossible to get through Freshers' Week without some mention (or several!) of alcohol but there are many activities that don't feature drinking and bars, so you need to seek those out. Not only is it *haram* to drink alcohol, it is also *haram* to buy it, give it as a gift or sit in a bar or pub, even if you are not drinking it.

Boyfriends and Girlfriends

The other aspect that you will see a lot of emphasis on in university is boys and girls in casual relationships. For some people this is the first time that they are in a mixed environment if they have been to a single sex school and there is a great deal of temptation to 'hook up' with someone just for the sake of not being left out.

Islam is quite categorical about the issue. There is no such thing as a girlfriend-boyfriend relationship. You are either married or you are single.

Just as it is our basic human need to eat, drink and sleep and so on, it is also our basic need to be loved and to be in a relationship that provides emotional as well as physical comfort. That is why Allah created Hawwa as a companion for Adam ﷺ so that they could live in peace and tranquillity together. Allah describes a husband and wife as being like a garment for one another (Surah Al-Baqarah 2:187). In other words, your life partner is someone who protects you, beautifies you, hides your faults - someone whom who are not complete without. To take such a beautiful, deep and life-long relationship and to reduce it to a casual physical encounter for a short period of time only to move onto the next one makes no sense at all.

But as we discussed earlier, in the societies we live in, Man has created his own laws and one of those is the freedom of the individual to do what he pleases as long as he isn't causing harm to anyone else. So the norm is for people to be in casual physical relationships with the opposite sex and even with the same sex, before they get married and even after they get married.

As human beings we only understand the concept of harm as it affects us. So if we are in a dozen casual but consenting relationships, where is the harm in that? What's the problem if we have a relationship with someone of the same sex? We're not hurting anyone else, are we?

But Allah in His wisdom understands that these actions are harmful to society as a whole and so individuals need to make small personal sacrifices in order to make the world around us a better place to be. The more harmful the action to society, the greater the punishment for doing it.

Zina (fornication or adultery) is about the most serious sin you can commit as a Muslim. Why so serious? I'll tell you why. When prioritising something or giving it a certain importance, we should consider the consequences of doing or not doing that thing. The penalty for adultery (for a married person) according to Islam is death as Ibn Masoud ☀ related that Prophet Muhammad ☀ said,

> *"The blood of a Muslim may not be legally spilt other than in one of three instances: the married person who commits adultery, a life for a life, and one who forsakes his religion and abandons the community."* (Bukhari and Muslim)

The Qur'an mentions the punishment for fornication (for an unmarried person):

> *A woman and a man who commit fornication: flog both of them with one hundred lashes and do not let compassion for either of them possess you where Allah's deen is concerned, if you have iman in Allah and the Last Day. A number of mu'minun should witness their punishment.* (Surah An-Nur 24:2)

> *And do not go near to fornication. It is an indecent act, an evil way.* (Surah Al-Isra 17:32)

Is it worth ruining your life in this world and the Next for something so evil?

Now the beauty of Islam, is that when something is *haram* then all the doors leading to it are also *haram*, which makes it easier for everyone to follow the rules. For example, if you tell a child that they can't eat sweets but everyone around them is eating sweets and there are sweets easily available everywhere, then that child will almost certainly eat sweets!

So everything that could lead to *zina* is also *haram*. Looking with desire at someone, laughing and joking with the opposite sex, being alone together with someone of the opposite sex, even if there is no physical contact are all *haram*. We are told in the *hadith* that when two unmarried persons are alone in each other's company, the third person is *Shaytan* who is whispering to them and tempting them with the forbidden (Tirmidhi). A lot of people will claim that they have platonic relationships with the opposite sex; that they can control themselves and simply enjoy each other's company. These thoughts and ideas are nothing but the whispers of *Shaytan*.

> *Repel the thought, for if you do not, it becomes an idea. So repel the idea, for if you do not it will become a desire. So fight against that (desire), for if you do not, it will become a determination and a passion. And if you do not repel that, it will become an action. And if you do not replace it with its opposite, it will become a constant habit. So at that point, it will be difficult for you to change it.* (Ibn Qayyim Al-Jawziyyah)

Step-by-Step Approach

It is worth spending a bit of time thinking about that last saying. We saw from Chapter 1 in the exchange that Iblis had with Allah when he refused to bow down to Adam ﷺ, that Iblis is determined to sway us from the right path and he will use any means he can to do so. A particularly effective tactic that he uses is the step-by-step approach. What do I mean by that?

You've just arrived in your halls of residence. A set of parents is dropping off their daughter at the same halls. Now you look like a decent kind of guy. Her parents are looking very nervous and ask you to keep an eye on her as she has never been away from home before. They trust you to look after her in their absence and so, of course, you reassure them that you will do your best. After all, that would be the kind thing to do and she'll make friends soon enough and then it's not your problem.

A couple of weeks pass and you haven't seen this girl. Now you remember what her parents asked you to do and so you and a couple of your friends approach her while she is with her friends in the common room and you ask her, without looking at her, if she's OK. She says, "Yeah" and you walk away.

As you're walking away you think, "That must have come across a bit rude. I'll go and apologise to her tomorrow." So you knock on the door of her room and she opens up. Standing outside her room, with her inside, you say, "Sorry about yesterday. I mean..er..if I sounded rude." "That's alright," she says with a smile.

A week later you meet her walking back from her department to the halls of residence. It's after dark, so you offer to walk back to halls with her. After all you wouldn't want your own sister walking around alone after dark and she is someone else's sister. You walk with her in silence but as you drop her off at the door of the hall building, she says that she would feel better if you could walk her home regularly in the evenings now that it gets dark early. You agree. You wouldn't want to be the reason that anything bad happened to the girl.

Now you begin walking back to the halls with her every day and every time she tries to make conversation, you give her a short answer. After a few days of doing this, you think, "I must come across as really rude. In fact she must think that all Muslim guys are like this. That's not a very good impression she will get of Muslims." So you start to get chatting. Nothing wrong in that, you think. You are in a public place.

She is doing one of the same courses as you are and she asks for your help one day with an assignment. After you've helped her with it, you're tired and hungry and don't have the energy to cook. So when she suggests going to the pizza place around the corner to grab something to eat, you don't say no. You spend more time there than you had anticipated. You miss your *Maghrib salah*. Never mind. You'll combine it with your *'Isha*. It's not the end of the world.

You find yourself enjoying this girl's company. She's fun, easy to be with and you have a good laugh. What's wrong with that? You're never in a secluded place together so nothing is ever going to happen. Anyway, you won't let things get THAT far.

But over the coming weeks you find yourself thinking less and less and being led more and more by your emotions. You've missed a few of your *salah*, but since Allah hasn't struck you down with a bolt of lightning, He can't be that mad. You stop going to the prayer room and hanging out with your Muslim mates, because you are spending more and more time with this girl.

And then one day, the inevitable happens. You've committed the major sin of *zina*, along with a whole host of other sins such as lying and not praying.

Shaytan has taken the step-by-step approach by slowly lowering your aversion to that which is bad so you don't feel so guilty. He also plants thoughts in your mind to make you think that the advice he is giving is sincere and in your best interest and then WHAM! One day you wake up and you have crossed the limits of Allah and you are not quite sure how you got there but *Shaytan* is the winner and you are the loser. If someone had said to you on the first day of term, "Stop praying, stop reading the Qur'an and sleep with a girl", you would never even have entertained that thought, but just a few months later, that's exactly what you have done.

Now I know you are thinking – that will never happen to me! But it only takes the most insignificant event or turn and you are on a slippery slope to a destination that you never even dreamed of. As Prophet Muhammad ﷺ said in his Last Sermon:

> *"Beware of Shaytan, for the safety of your religion. He has lost all hope that he will ever be able to lead you astray in big things, so beware of following him in small things."*

Haya *or Modesty*

We would not be human if we didn't feel tempted once in a while. Success does not lie in never feeling desire for something inappropriate, it is in restraining those desires for the pleasure of Allah. Think of the immense rewards for doing so.

One of the most valued qualities in Islam is modesty and we need to feel it, especially around the opposite sex. It acts as a shield and protects us from doing wrong. Abdullah ibn Umar ؓ narrated that the Prophet ﷺ said:

> *"Indeed haya and iman are companions. When one of them is lifted, the other leaves as well."* (Bayhaqi)

This is not only an excellent quality to have, but an essential one and one can never have enough of it. This is something to especially remember in these times when 'moral' and 'modest' are portrayed as 'backward', 'oppressed' and 'under-confident'. Furthermore, lacking modesty is one of the reasons cited as being a cause for encountering difficulties in life.

> *Five things are associated with difficulty in life: a hardened heart, eyes that don't shed tears, limited haya, desire for the material world, and having lengthy hopes/desires in your life.*
> (Al-Fudayl ibn 'Iyad)

Jannah *is Surrounded by Difficult Things*

Shaytan has many tricks up his sleeve. Taking the step-by-step approach is just one of them. Another strategy he has is to make wrong actions seem attractive and appealing and easy to do. But in fact these may lead us to *Jahannum* and what looks like something not worth doing or actions that seem too difficult to do could in fact take us into *Jannah*.

> *A calamity that makes you turn to Allah is better for you than a blessing which makes you forget the remembrance of Allah.*
> (Ibn Taymiyyah)

Jahannum is surrounded by tempting things and sin appears attractive to us. On the other hand, *Jannah* is surrounded by difficult things such as sharing wealth, exercising self-control and sacrifice.

Shade on a Hot Day

Last week I was walking along and I saw something which made me think. I saw a mature lady walking down the road holding up an opened umbrella. There was nothing dramatic or striking about the lady or the umbrella. The point is there wasn't a drop of rain to be seen as the skies were clear and it was a warm day. The lady was using the umbrella to provide her shade from the sun.

Here on Earth, we are millions of miles away from the sun yet on a hot day we find it unbearable to be in the sun and find ways to protect ourselves from its heat. But what about the Day of Judgement when it is reported that the sun will be so close to us that people will be drowning in their sweat? On that day there will be no shade except for those whom Allah grants shade under His Throne.

Who will be awarded this shade? The following *hadith* informs us of ways we can try to qualify for this shade. It was reported by Abu Huraira ﷜ that the Prophet ﷺ said:

> *"There are seven whom Allah will shade with His shade on the day when there will be no shade except His: the just ruler; a young man who grows up worshipping his Lord; a man whose heart is attached to the mosque; two men who love one another for the sake of Allah and meet and part on that basis; a man who is called by a woman of rank and beauty and says 'I fear Allah'; a man who gives in charity and conceals it to such an extent that his left hand does not know what his right hand gives; and a man who remembers Allah when he is alone, and his eyes fill up."* (Bukhari and Muslim)

This *hadith* mentions the seven categories of people who will be granted shade on that day. One of those is a young person who spends their youth in worship of Allah and the other is the person who is tempted by someone of the opposite sex but refuses.

Two Wings of A Bird

It's very easy to despair and fall into the trap of thinking that Allah is just waiting to punish our every wrong action and being overly fearful of Him. Fear of Allah is a good thing but we should not just feel fear when we think of Allah otherwise we will become pessimistic and fall into despair.

On the other hand, it is equally easy to become complacent and hope that we will be forgiven for all our sins no matter what they are without actually doing anything. That would be deceiving ourselves and clinging onto a false hope.

We need to strike a balance and remain between fear of Allah's punishment and hope of His mercy. People have described these two interdependent qualities as two wings of a bird. You need both of them to fly. Allah has praised the people of hope and fear in the following verse:

> *Is one who worships devoutly during the hours of the night, prostrating himself or standing (in adoration), who takes heed of the Hereafter and who places his hope in the mercy of his Lord – (like one who does not)?* (Surah Az-Zumar 39:9)

The Importance of a Good Start

Being in the construction industry, I understand fully how important the foundations are to any building. In fact doing the ground work on most construction sites is usually the most difficult part but once the foundations have been laid properly the rest of the structure goes up pretty easily in comparison.

Similarly, if you want to get the most out of university then you need to get going right from the very start. If you can get the hang of taking the initiative early on in your studies, you will find that you are on top of the study schedule and not under pressure to continually catch up. Also if you start as you mean to go on, then the early days of your university life will define your time there socially, academically and in terms of overall attitude. Make informed and responsible decisions early on and they will put you in the best possible position for the rest of your time at university.

The same applies to life in general. It is tempting to think that there is plenty of time to gain religious knowledge or perform acts of worship and to concentrate solely on matters of the *dunya* in our youth. But if we work hard to ground ourselves in authentic knowledge of the *deen* and worship to the very best of our ability early on in life then not only will we gain extra reward for it (see the *hadith* about Shade on the Day of Judgement above) but for the rest of our lives we will be well-equipped to deal with whatever comes our way, *insha'Allah*. Our desire for the *dunya* is a lot stronger when we are young and we have peer pressure pushing us to get up to all sorts but once we hit middle and old age, then naturally these worldly desires will diminish. If we can establish the obligatory prayers in our youth rather than a routine of hitting the nightclubs and choose to remain chaste rather than being promiscuous then no doubt we will get a great reward from Allah for our patience.

Have the Right Intentions

One of the most important things in Islam is not only the actions that we perform, but also the intentions that we have before we carry them out. If you think about it, you have to make an intention before you do anything such as *salah* or fasting, so it must be pretty important. Allah will only reward us for our efforts when we do deeds for His pleasure alone. That means that we should not do good deeds for recognition, for praise or for reward from other human beings. After all, why should Allah reward us for something we did not intend to do for Him in the first place?

Perhaps a great deed is belittled by an intention and perhaps a small deed, by a sincere intention, is made great. (Abdullah ibn Al-Mubarak)

'Umar ibn al-Khattab ؓ reported that the Messenger of Allah ﷺ said:

> *"The deeds are considered by the intentions, and a person will get the reward according to his intention. So whoever emigrated for Allah and His Messenger, his emigration will be for Allah and His Messenger; and whoever emigrated for worldly benefits or for a woman to marry, his emigration would be for what he emigrated for."* (Bukhari and Muslim)

On the basis of this *hadith*, the scholars are of the unanimous opinion that the real basis of one's actions is *niyyah* (intention) and everyone will be rewarded or punished according to his *niyyah*. In other words, in every righteous deed one should seek only the pleasure of Allah, otherwise it will not be accepted by Allah.

Deeds without sincerity are like a traveller who carries in his water-jug dirt. The carrying of it burdens him and it brings no benefit. (Ibn Qayyim Al Jawziyyah)

Learning

The one key area in which university is very different from school is in the nature of the teaching process. You will very quickly come to realise that lecturers are not school teachers and large impersonal lecture theatres are not small intimate classrooms. No matter how well you performed at school, you will have to completely change the way you learn if you want to be successful at university.

You will have much less contact with your lecturers than you did with your teachers and you can expect far less input from them both in terms of actually teaching you what you need to know and also how you are doing. Obviously the exact teaching style will depend on your course and your university but in general you are in charge of your own education now and you have to play an active role in learning.

Does that sound scary? Well this is how it works. Think of attending a lecture as a briefing. Your lecturer will tell you about a particular topic and maybe give you a handout with a reading list. This is your starting point or springboard to find out more about that topic. The lecture may be followed up with a tutorial in which you are given problem sheets. If you have simply just listened to the lecture and nothing else, then you will have a hard time answering any of the problem sheet questions, and that doesn't bode too well for your exams.

Now, with all due respect to lecturers, it can be very hard to listen to someone speaking about the Jacobian determinant formed from the n^2 differential coefficients of n given functions of n independent variables, without falling asleep. This is where note-taking becomes a valuable practice. It turns the passive act of listening to a lecture (with the danger of words going in one ear and out of the other) into an active involvement on your part. You can choose to write notes straight onto a fresh sheet of paper or to annotate the handout from the lecturer. Either way you will (hopefully) stay focused throughout the lecture and have a valuable resource to refer to when you come to revise.

And finally, do bear in mind that...

Knowledge is that which benefits, not that which is memorised.
(Imam Ash-Shafi'i)

It's up to you to focus on your studies and ensure that you are on top of your workload. Again, the extent of this varies, but you probably won't receive much supervision and if you fall behind you can't depend on anyone else to catch up for you. If you start to find things too difficult or slip behind, only you can do something about it. Unless you act, the problem is only going to get worse so don't be afraid to ask for help from friends, other students on the course and, of course, your lecturers.

This pattern of self-learning and self-motivation will carry you well through life. When we were young, our parents probably sent us to the *masjid* to learn the Qur'an and we had no choice in the matter. As we get older, that is no longer the case and we are pretty much left alone to decide whether we want to continue to learn about the religion and how we wish to do that.

Just as study is the priority at university, then Islam should be the priority in life. We can help ourselves do well by keeping in good, pious company and studying about the *deen* both on our own and within a gathering. There is a *hadith* that if we remember Allah in a gathering then Allah remembers us in a bigger and better gathering – in other words, with the angels (Tabarani).

Ignoring religion in the prime of life would be like not studying at all for the first half of the course. If you want to succeed, you have to put in the hours regularly and right from the start.

Personal Motivation

Because no one is going to hold you to account for how many lectures you attended and whether you did the extra reading or not, you are going to have to be accountable to yourself. It's quite hard to maintain a high level of motivation for every day of the three or four or five year course that you are on. So what do you do on the days that you just can't face getting out of bed on a cold morning and walking in the rain to get to a 9am lecture?

The key is to think of your long term goal and you must be clear in your mind what that is. If you want status and a high salary, then you will need the best job in your field. That means you are going to need to get the best degree possible and you are not going to get that by lying around in bed. The mental image of sitting in your plush office with your name engraved on the door should be enough to get you out of bed and in the front row of that lecture theatre at 9am sharp!

Now I am not saying that these material considerations are the best goals to have in life, but my point is that everybody is motivated by something and that spurs them onto act NOW. All those little steps that you take will lead you to your final destination, whatever you choose that to be.

So the next time you are lying in bed and you know that you ought to do your *Fajr salah* but cannot get up to do *wudu* in the cold, you have to think of your long term goal and whether the way you are acting right now is helping you towards that goal or hindering it. The whole point of our life here on earth is to seek the pleasure of Allah and entry into *Jannah*. Lying in bed will not move us closer to that but performing *Fajr* will. So there you have your answer about what you should do. If that doesn't work then think about the consequences of NOT doing the action. If you imagine Hellfire then that is sure to do the trick!

Of course, there are inspirational *ahadith*, scholars' sayings and books that you can turn to to help keep you motivated, to keep fresh in your mind the ultimate goal and to get you through the tough days.

Seeking knowledge is of tremendous importance in Islam. Of course that primarily refers to Islamic knowledge but it also means that we should gain knowledge of the world around us and use that to help other people, whether that is through medicine, engineering, law or one of the many other subjects.

The following is a *hadith* which I hope will keep you motivated during your time at university to gain both worldly and religious knowledge. Abu'd-Darda reported that the Messenger of Allah said:

> *"He who follows a path in quest of knowledge, Allah will make the path of Jannah easy for him. The angels lower their wings over the seeker of knowledge, being pleased with what he does. The inhabitants of the heavens and the earth*

and even the fish in the depths of the oceans seek forgiveness for him. The superiority of the learned man over the devout worshipper is like that of the full moon to the rest of the stars (i.e., in brightness). The learned are the heirs of the Prophets who bequeath neither dinar nor dirham but only that of knowledge; and he who acquires it, has in fact acquired an abundant portion." (Abu Dawud and Tirmidhi)

While learning at university, as long as you have the intention in the back of your mind that you are looking to obtain the pleasure of Allah by seeking knowledge then, *insha'Allah*, you will be rewarded for every lecture you attend and every bit of effort you make towards your studies.

New Friendships

People will start forming groups of friends as soon as they arrive. Some of these new friendships won't last past Freshers' Week and others will stay strong for the whole university course and beyond. Again, personally speaking, the friends that I made in Freshers' week stuck with me throughout my university years and we have still stayed in touch years later.

So how do you know whether the person you have just been chatting to in the course registration queue for the past ten minutes goes on to become a lifelong friend or someone whom you never see again? Well of course you can never know. But a good indicator is whether you have the same approach to studies, socialising and life in general. If you plan to work hard, attend all the lectures, stay away from distractions such as drinking and clubbing, then it's best to hang around those people who support your ethics. By all means you should be friendly with everyone that you meet, but do be choosy about whom you call a friend and choose to spend time with. It's no exaggeration to say that it will have a big effect on your academic career.

If you have not been able to become a part of a group or you have not found people that you are comfortable with, don't let it stop you enjoying yourself. You will find those people. They may not be in your halls or classes and you may need to cast the net wider to find them. Just think logically about where to find your kind of people. Hopefully one of your 'interests' will or should be Islam. Most universities will have an Islamic Society or something similar. They will have a prayer room where you can not only meet other people but also get your prayers done. For men, attending the *Jumu'ah* (Friday congregational) prayer on campus is also a good starting point.

Find a Good Seat

It might seem trivial but it is important where and whom you sit with in the lecture theatre. In fact, it's worth turning up a couple of minutes earlier to a lecture to find yourself a good seat (and I don't mean somewhere where you can curl up and go to sleep!). There are some things to consider as you decide where to sit.

Lecturers are always a little bit wary of the group that sits right at the back. It gives the impression that the student is not interested and students have been known to get up to all sorts in the back row! That doesn't mean to say you have to sit under the lecturer's nose either, but choose a spot where you can see the lecturer and are able to read his notes on the blackboard/whiteboard/screen clearly.

You also need to be able to hear what the lecturer is saying, and that will not be possible if you are sitting in the middle of a group of people who are using the lecture time to catch up on the latest gossip. If you need to get up and move away then do so, without worrying about what other people will think. After all, it's your time and money being spent, so spend it wisely.

The First Year in General

Although students may be required to achieve a minimum percentage pass mark in order to progress on to the next year of their studies, the first year usually does not count much (or sometimes not at all) towards the final degree.

This means that some students take this as a licence to enjoy themselves and not take the first year seriously. However, I would advise you not to overlook your first year and do not underestimate its importance.

Firstly, you develop the fundamentals and the foundations for your subject in your first year: both in terms of study skills and in terms of actual course material. If that foundation is weak then you struggle in the later years.

On top of that, your first year *can* be looked up by future employers, and most definitely will be for internship applications submitted at the end of the first year or the beginning of your second year.

To sum up, these early days are an exciting time of change and new experiences. It is very easy to get caught up in the excitement and lose sight of the reason for being at university. However, if you can start on the right track both in terms of your studies and also your social life, then *insha'Allah*, you will have laid a good foundation for the rest of your time at university.

Chapter 3

Guidance and Learning

As we saw in the previous chapter, the onus is more on you to succeed at university. The resources are at your disposal but it is up to you to make the best of them. Your long-term success depends very much on your nature and how you choose to act now.

Different Types of People

You will find a spectrum of different types of people at university, even on the same course, but I think they can neatly be categorised into three groups:

There are the people that relax and enjoy themselves to the max. They are so busy enjoying themselves that even if they make it past the first and second years, they are bound to fail the course. Now we'll call these guys the 'Chilled Out' bunch.

Then you have the people that enjoyed their first year to the max like the 'Chilled Out' guys but then they realised that in order to pass they would have to put in the hours. So they do the work in the later years, especially close to the exams, and get through with respectable results. These guys, we'll call the 'Catch Up' students.

And finally there is the 'Smart' bunch and I wanted to be one of them. They worked hard and they played hard. You would find them attending every lecture and tutorial but after hours they were also enjoying themselves in the pool room, the student union café or the courtyard. These guys were having the time of their life and getting top marks in all the coursework and exams. If you work hard and smart (in other words efficiently) then there is no reason why you can't be one of these students and enjoy everything that university life has to offer.

But being smart does not begin and end at university and with academic life. There are lots of 'Chilled Out' Muslims. These people believe in Allah but haven't grasped the purpose of their existence, don't do anywhere near what is required of them to do in order to succeed in the test of life and live their lives satisfying their whims and desires. Subsequently, they end up failing the biggest test of all.

I see that some people are content with the least of the deen, but I do not see them pleased with meagerness in this life.
(Abdullah ibn Al-Mubarak)

The 'Catch Up' Muslims enjoy their youth and don't pay a great deal of attention to religious matters. They realise that they ought to be 'better' Muslims but count on the fact that they will 'catch up' in their middle or old age and by then will hopefully have done enough to earn a place in *Jannah*.

Now a 'Smart' Muslim is, in my opinion, better described as a *mu'min*. This is the top grade Muslim, who is focused on his goal from the outset. He understands what he has to do and does it and spends a great deal of time increasing his knowledge. He desires his goal more than the 'Catch Up' Muslim; the thought of failure petrifies him a lot more than the 'Chilled Out' Muslim and his level of *iman* is more than the other two put together.

Having read the descriptions of the three categories of students, you probably want to aim to be a 'Smart' student and excel in your studies and have a great social life. In the same way, we should all aim to be *mu'mins* and not just 'Chilled Out' or 'Catch Up' Muslims. In both cases, as 'Smart' students and 'Smart' Muslims, you need to choose appropriate friends who will help and encourage you and you need to make the best use of the resources that are available to you in order to be successful.

Choosing Friends Wisely

To satisfy our need for interaction and socialisation with others, we make friends and we need to choose our friends wisely if we want to succeed in life. This is beautifully illustrated in the following *hadith* where Abu Musa Al-Ash'ari ﷺ reported:

> *"I heard the Prophet ﷺ saying, 'The similitude of good company and that of bad company is that of the owner of musk and of the one blowing the bellows. The owner of musk would either offer you some free of charge, or you would buy it from him, or you smell its pleasant fragrance; and as for the one who blows the bellows (i.e. the blacksmith), he either burns your clothes or you smell a repugnant smell.'"* (Bukhari and Muslim)

Have you ever walked through the perfume section of a department store and noticed that you smell of perfume when you get home, even though you did not put any on? Whether you want to or not, you will pick up the scent. Likewise, if you associate yourselves with hard working students ('Smart' people) you will stand to gain all the time and ultimately become like them. On days that you feel less motivated to study or to pray, your 'Smart' friends will be there to boost your confidence and remind you of your goal and you will be there for them when they need you. Having 'Chilled Out' friends may seem like more fun initially, but they will not help you focus on what is important and in the end, it will be you who loses out.

Teamwork

You will find on your course timetable that there are opportunities for you to work by yourself as well in groups with other people. That is because both skills are important. Likewise, some acts of worship are individual such as fasting while others are collective such as the *Jumu'ah salah*. This shows that the nature of Islam is not just about the individual but also about brotherhood/sisterhood and the necessity of interacting positively with others.

Whether you are working in pairs or groups of twenty and whatever the task, the same basic principles for successful teamwork apply. The first thing is to realise that each person will bring to the team differing skills and personalities. The trick is to identify everyone's strengths and to work to those, while compensating for each other's weaknesses, so that the team is strong as a unit and there is harmony among the team members.

The other critical element of teamwork success is that all the team efforts are directed towards the same clear goals, the team goals. This relies heavily on a common vision and good communication between the team members. Each team member must be clear about what his or her role is and what they are responsible for. Each team therefore needs a leader to ensure the smooth running of the team, to direct the members and oversee the flow of communication.

Developing a Good Relationship with your Lecturers

You may have less interaction with your lecturers and tutors than you did with your teachers at school, but that doesn't mean that they should just remain names and faces that you listen to in lectures and then leave.

In later years, you may need your lecturers' help with your final year project and dissertation, career's advice, and to act as referees for jobs and work placements. So do make sure that you are on good terms with the staff in your department. You may be assigned a personal tutor to whom you can go if you need to discuss any issues. Even if you don't have any problems, then it is still worth maintaining a good relationship with them and making the time to visit them regularly. You never know when they could be useful.

The other key difference between school and university is how the exam system works. While at school you will have sat national exams that were set and marked by external examiners. At university, the lecturers write the syllabus, the course (sometimes the text books as well!) and of course, they write and mark your exams and award you the degree. So even if you are doing the same course as someone in a different university you may be studying quite different things.

The problem with this system is that there is no one text book or revision guide that will contain all you need to know for your final exams. You have to build up your own course folder using the lecture handouts, your lecture notes, your supplementary notes from your extra reading as well as any problem sheets/assignments. It is up to you to add to it as necessary so that you have a complete resource from which to revise come exam time.

Now although that sounds very illogical and inconvenient, you can actually use that to your advantage. Every time you attend a lecture, you are looking at and listening to the person who will be marking your exam paper for that subject! Listen to the tips they give you about what is important and what is not, get hold of the text books that they recommend, work out what their style is. If they like to see diagrams to accompany explanations and equations derived from first principles, then that is what you need to do.

So listen carefully to what your lecturers are saying and do bear in mind that you are not just another face in the lecture theatre to them. They will be aware of your attendance, your diligence in lectures and so ensure that they have a good impression of you.

The Ultimate Role Model

If you think back over your academic life, there will probably be one teacher that stands out as being particularly good. Why? Maybe they were able to relate to you, speak in the kind of language that you understood, were on the same wavelength as you. This teacher not only knew their subject well but could explain it well and probably made an effort to make learning enjoyable. In turn you enjoyed that subject and did better at it.

Allah has sent 125,000 prophets over the history of mankind. Some of them had a revised message to convey and others conveyed the previous message that had been forgotten. But whenever a nation had fallen into wrongdoing and disobeying the commands of the Creator, then Allah sent guidance in the form of a prophet. Allah chose these prophets as being the best people to convey the message to their nation. They were humble, eloquent men who had the most noble character but were from among the people and understood them and knew how to speak to them.

When Allah felt that mankind was ready to receive the final message then he revealed the Qur'an through his chosen final Messenger, Muhammad ﷺ. The Prophet Muhammad ﷺ knew his subject inside out, in fact he was (and still is) the best example of how a human being should be. He demonstrated with every aspect of his life how to truly live Islam. A more perfect role model than Prophet Muhammad ﷺ for all time and places will never be found. He is, as his wife, the Mother of the Believers, A'ishah ﷺ described him, the 'Qur'an in motion'.

You have an excellent model in the Messenger of Allah, for all those who put their hope in Allah and the Last Day and remember Allah much. (Surah Al-Ahzab 33:21)

We need to be clear that Prophet Muhammad ﷺ addressed contemporary issues relevant to the youth and that the guidance in the Qur'an and the teachings of our beloved Prophet ﷺ are not out-dated or irrelevant to modern times. Our realities may be different but as human beings, what has changed over the years? Our wants, needs and desires are the same and Islam today has an answer for every possible question and situation that may arise. As Allah Himself says in the Qur'an:

> *This day, I have perfected your religion for you, completed My Favour upon you, and have chosen for you Islam as your religion.* (Surah Al-Maidah 5:3)

Whatever stage of life or situation you are in, you will find something in the Prophet's life that you can take from. He was a son, a spouse, a parent, a student of knowledge, a leader, a good friend and an ambassador of Islam. He bore the loss of his parents, his grandfather and uncle, his children and his wife. He endured the displeasure of his fellow citizens (they threw stones at his feet until he bled and tried to kill him in his bed), but throughout all of that he was always abundantly grateful to Allah and kind and just to everyone, friend or enemy.

There are a number of biographies of the Prophet ﷺ (*Seerah*) available from the simple to the very detailed, some concentrating on the events of that period, others on the character of the Prophet ﷺ. In any case, I think that the *Seerah* is an essential read for any student of Islam in order to get an idea of what a noble human being is and how we can go some way to become one.

Prioritising

With so much to do, the key to getting it all done in time is to establish a list of priorities and assign every task a level of importance and urgency. Then you have to spend time getting the important and urgent tasks done first and leave the things that are neither important nor urgent. It's simple if, for each task, you consider the potential consequences of doing it or leaving it.

Something that is important will have significant consequences to your studies and likewise, something that is not important will have few or no consequences or significance to your studies. The very worst use of your time is to do something well and then realise that it did not need to be done at all!

By extension, it is a very useful concept to carry right through your life in all your activities that to achieve the most, you need to concentrate on the small number of activities that contribute the greatest value to your goal. In order to get our priorities right, we first need to know what they are or should be so that we don't waste our time doing what we think is worth doing to later realise that it was a complete waste of time.

The main fact that we need to bear in mind about our existence on earth, is that it is temporary and the Hereafter is what really counts. Allah explains in the Qur'an:

> Know that the life of the dunya is merely a game and a diversion and ostentation an a cause of boasting among yourselves and trying to outdo one another in wealth and children: like the plant-growth after rain which delights the cultivators, but then it withers and you see it turning yellow, and then it becomes broken stubble. In the akhirah there is terrible punishment but also forgiveness from Allah and His good pleasure. The life of the dunya is nothing but the enjoyment of delusion.
> (Surah Al-Hadid 57:20)

Or in the words of a Companion:

> You build that which you will not live in; you work and work and you die in them. You gather up that which you will not consume and you have hopes which you will never have. The people before you got deceived by the dunya so they gathered up homes and wealth...and all it did was take them away from the akhirah. (Abu'd-Darda')

This idea is repeated several times throughout the Qur'an because Allah knows that we are weak and narrow-minded and we cannot grasp the concept that this world simply isn't worth anything.

Yet you still prefer the life of the dunya when the akhirah is better and longer lasting. (Surah Al-A'la 87:16-17)

The Prophet Muhammad ﷺ gave us a wonderful visual example of the worth of this world in the following *hadith* reported by Jabir ibn 'Abdullah ﵁:

The Messenger of Allah ﷺ happened to walk through the bazaar coming from the side of 'Aliya and people were on both sides of him. There he found a dead lamb with very short ears. He took hold of its ear and said: "Who amongst you would like to have this for a dirham?" They said: "We would not like to have it even for less than that as it is of no use to us." He said: "Do you wish to have it (free of any cost)?" They said: "By Allah, even if it were alive (we would not have liked to possess it), for there is defect in it, as its ear is very short; on top of that it is dead now." Thereupon, the Prophet ﷺ said: "By Allah, this world is more insignificant in the eyes of Allah than (this dead lamb) is in your eyes." (Muslim)

Scholars throughout the ages have also understood the worth of the world and compared it to a shadow or a dream:

O people who take pleasure in a life that will vanish, falling in love with a fading shadow is sheer stupidity.
(Ibn Qayyim Al Jawziyyah)

What is this world but a dream that a sleeper sees - he delights in it for a few moments, and then wakes up to face reality.
(Al-Hasan Al-Basri)

In order to be successful we need to grasp that the few decades we are on earth are nothing in comparison to the eternity of the Hereafter and that the world we love so much is not worth anything at all in the great scheme of things. Think about how much time and energy we spend worrying about things that in the eyes of Allah are neither important nor urgent and how little we actually worry about the Hereafter, which is extremely important and urgent.

The world is three days: as for yesterday, it has vanished along with all that was in it. As for tomorrow, you may never see it. As for today, it is yours, so work on it. (Al-Hasan Al-Basri)

Islam has placed upon us obligations (*arkan*), for example *salah* and fasting, and as a bare minimum we need to strive to fulfil these obligations to the best of our ability. In order to do that, we need to plan and arrange our lifestyles accordingly.

For example, if your lecturer told you that you would pass your course by turning up to five lectures a day on time for every single day of the course, you would be stupid if you watched TV or slept through them. Now when Allah tells us to perform *salah* five times every day, we find other things take priority. I grew up in a house where drama serials were taken very seriously and for years I would be watching TV when the time for prayer arrived. Of course, once the drama finished, so too did the time for *salah*.

If we fully understand the purpose of life, are clear about what our end goals are and how to achieve them, then there would be no question of us doing the things that are neither important nor urgent and ignoring the things that are!

Turning Up Would Help

Just as *salah* forms the basis of a Muslim's day, so lectures and tutorials are the backbone of the course. The fact is, if you don't attend your lectures and tutorials, you will fall behind rapidly. You should aim to attend each and every one of these on time and fully prepared with whatever the lecturer may have asked you do beforehand. It is not an option to miss something without a good reason.

It is tempting to dismiss the very first lecture of a subject as a wasted hour where the lecturer will not cover much ground. But often these are the very lectures where you can gain an insight into the lecturer's personality, the aims, objectives and structure of the course, which can be a great foundation for the rest of the year.

Getting your friend to give you the lecture handout is not a substitute for actually attending the lecture. The handout just has a few pointers about what the lecture covered but if you want those all important tips and recommendations from the lecturer about what is important and where to go for the extra reading then you will have to attend the lecture.

I will never forget a presentation I did as a group in one of my modules in the first year. I attended the first couple of lectures of the module and collected the handout which gave an outline of a presentation we were to do. Our group of friends missed the next few lectures as we were busy tuning up our pool skills in the Student Union café!

We prepared our presentation using the instructions of the handout and on presentation day, we were first up on stage, confidently presenting our work. The other students and lecturer all had a smile on their face, so we thought we had done rather well. When all the other groups had finished their presentations, it dawned on us that the lecturer had explained in detail what he wanted to see in the presentation and what he would be marking us on in the two lectures we had missed and that the students were not smiling at us, they were laughing at our mistakes!

The moral of the story is simple. Attend all your lectures!

Getting Organised

Being organised is a really easy way to improve your grades and reduce stress in the future, and if you're doing it from day one it can become virtually effortless. Decide on a routine and stick to it literally from your first lecture. Later on in the year, when you are looking through your notes to revise from, everything will be in order and you will be able to find what you are looking for easily and quickly.

Starting from the very first introductory lecture, do ensure that you keep the handouts, problem sheets and your own notes complete and in order. Your notes should be legible and don't forget to write out the references of the books you have used to make your notes. There is nothing worse than reading through your notes later and not knowing which book you took them from. It will save you an enormous amount of pre-exam time and worry if you can keep a complete and ordered course folder. The lever arch file and divider system is just one method of keeping organised. It worked for me and in fact I have adopted this method in my professional life in the office and it's still working for me. However, as long as you know how it works and are able to access what you need, then use whatever filing system suits you.

I personally found that the state of my room reflected my state of mind. If my desk and room were in a tidy state and everything was in its place, then I would generally be on top of things and in a pretty relaxed state of mind. However, at times my room became a tip. I couldn't find my notes, the desk was covered in paperwork and I found it difficult to focus mentally on anything. I would suggest that you maintain your desk and room in a way that enhances your productivity, clarity and focus. Your surroundings affect you deeply – probably more than you realise. Your room doesn't have to look like a sterile laboratory with everything at perfect right angles, but if you can't see the colour of the carpet and there is a pizza under your bed with a fuzzy green-coloured topping, then it may be time for a clear-up.

It is also a good idea to have a diary or some similar set up that enables you to record where you need to be and when, as well as any deadlines. This is vital if you want to organise and prioritise your time. There'll be too much to remember so it must be with you almost all the time. You can choose something as simple as a pen-and-paper diary or the latest Smartphone. Personally, my phone is all I need to keep organised and without it I'm lost!

Work Smarter, Not Harder

There is a saying that 'You only get out what you put in'. In general that is true, but good results are not just down to effort. You may hear people saying that they have done a certain number of hours of revision or that they stayed awake all night doing a project. They may have put the hours in, but that does not automatically translate into good marks. The questions you need to ask yourself before you embark on an assignment or sit down to revise are: Am I working on the most important material? Am I practising the problems that are most likely to come up in the exam? Am I taking in the information that will help me? Am I spending too long on something that does not yield that many marks? There is no doubt that without effort you do not achieve results, but that effort must be directed in an intelligent and well-planned manner.

You need to be critical and constantly assess whether the work you are doing will get you the grades that you need. It helps to refer to previous exam papers to see what the style of questions are. How many marks are allocated to what parts of the question? For example, there is no point learning equations if they are given to you on the exam paper and little point in just stating the right answer if almost all the marks are given for the working out!

Worship Smarter, Not Longer

Allah tells us in the Qur'an in no uncertain terms what our purpose in life is:

> *I have only created and jinns that they may serve me.*
> (Surah Adh-Dhariyat 56:51)

Just as at university, once we know what our task is we need to know how we go about completing that task to the best of our ability. Similarly, we now need to ask ourselves how do we fulfil our purpose in life and constantly worship Allah to the best of our ability?

It probably occurs to you (as it did to me) that constantly worshipping Allah means praying all day and night, fasting every day and never getting married. In fact, three men during the time of the Prophet ﷺ had the same idea and they came to him as the following *hadith* explains:

> *Anas ibn Malik ﷺ said, "Three people came to the houses of the wives of the Prophet ﷺ to ask about how the Prophet worshipped. When they were told, it was as if they thought it was little and said, 'Where are we in relation to the Messenger of Allah ﷺ, who has been forgiven his past and future wrong actions?' He said, 'One of them said, 'I will pray all of every night.' Another said, 'I will fast all the time and not break the fast.' The other said, 'I will withdraw from women and never marry.' The Messenger of Allah came to them and said, 'Are you the ones who said such-and-such? By Allah, I am the one among you with the most fear and awareness of Allah, but I fast and break the fast, I pray and I sleep, and I marry women. Whoever disdains my sunnah is not with me.'"* (Agreed upon)

In other words the Prophet Muhammad ﷺ maintained a balance between Allah's rights and his worldly duties. In fact the worldly duties, if done in accordance with the Qur'an and *Sunnah* and with the right intention, also count as worship. Visiting the sick is worship, greeting your fellow brother or sister with *salaam* and smiling at them is worship, removing a stone from the path so that it does not harm others is worship. Even sneezing and bathing are acts of worship when you remember Allah and the list is endless. There are many things that we can do and at times we don't do because we feel they are insignificant or we don't realise the great reward for doing these actions. In other words, our entire time in this world can be spent working for the Hereafter, without neglecting any of our worldly duties.

> *O youth! Seek the Hereafter, for we often see people pursuing the Hereafter and finding it as well as the dunya, but we have never seen anyone pursue the dunya and gain the Hereafter as well as the dunya.* (Al-Hasan Al-Basri)

Knowledge comes from Allah

Regardless of the number of hours you put in or how efficiently you try to work, it is important to remember that ultimately all knowledge comes to us from Allah. It is Allah Who has blessed us with our minds and given us the ability and opportunity to seek knowledge. The following Qur'anic *du'a* is a good one to repeat often:

> *My Lord! Increase me in knowledge.* (Surah Ta-Ha 20:114)

We must also remember that in seeking knowledge we should not neglect the commandments of Allah. For example, there are a number of students who miss the obligatory fasts of Ramadan, making the excuse that it would interfere with their study or exams.

In fact, you'll find that without the distraction of lunchtime during Ramadan, you have more time to devote to your studies. Having lunch at university for me was a social activity which took at least an hour and sometimes more by the time I had met up with all my friends, decided on where to eat, made our way there, decided on what to eat and then just having a chit chat after the meal. During

Ramadan, I had an 'extra' hour or two every day that I could use (or should have done!) for study.

Allah does not burden a soul with more than it can handle so if we have been commanded to fast and the exam season happens to be beckoning then so be it. *Insha'Allah*, Allah will help the student who does not neglect their worship in comparison to the one who does. Having said that, you still have to study as best you can. Knowledge will not come to you in your sleep as a miraculous reward for fasting during the exam season! The point is to keep both study and *ibadah* in perspective and not neglect either one.

Seeking Knowledge

Gaining knowledge does not end when your course at university finishes. Most graduates in their respective positions need to acquire further skills or pass professional exams usually in the form of Continuing Professional Development (CPD) so that their skills and knowledge are always up to date. In addition, most professionals become members of their relevant profession's society or institute after they graduate. These institutes publish regular subject journals and organise seminars that members can attend to keep abreast of what is happening in the field as well as providing the opportunity to meet like-minded people.

If we want to continually develop our self and our soul in order to become better human beings, then we need to continue to seek knowledge throughout our lives. As the Prophet Muhammad ﷺ said:

> *"To acquire knowledge is the duty of every Muslim man and woman."* (Ibn Majah)

Does that mean that once you have obtained your degree, you will have fulfilled your duty to acquire knowledge? Not quite. You may have become a good scientist or historian, but if you have not acquired the basic knowledge about religious obligations, you will remain an uneducated person. Today, there are millions of Muslims who have many degrees and a string of letters after their name and are very capable in their respective fields. However, it is all worthless if they have not even learnt to read the Qur'an or perform *salah*, let alone knowing how to conduct themselves as Muslims in their daily home, business and social lives.

All humans are dead except those who have knowledge. And all those who have knowledge are asleep, except those who do good deeds. And those who do good deeds are deceived, except those who are sincere. And those who are sincere are always in a state of worry. (Imam Ash-Shafi'i)

This tells us that knowledge in itself is not enough. It has to be accompanied by good deeds and sincere intentions. Our Qur'ans should not be sitting wrapped up in cloth on our bookshelves unread and not understood. That would be like expecting to pass your course by just buying the course textbook! It is beneficial knowledge that we should look to seek and when we acquire it, our actions should reflect it.

When a young man is devout, we don't recognise him by his speech. We recognise him by his actions. That is beneficial knowledge. (Al-Hasan Al-Basri)

Does this mean that every individual Muslim must also become a religious scholar? Not at all. We are required to seek knowledge to the best of our ability and circumstances and have sufficient knowledge to enable us to carry out our religious obligations. Knowledge of the *deen* gives us knowledge of the reality of this world, of the Hereafter, of Allah and what pleases and displeases Him. Acting sincerely upon this knowledge, therefore, should bring us closer to *Jannah*.

Seeking knowledge can have its pitfalls if done for the wrong reason. The Prophet ﷺ said:

> *"Do not attain learning in order to express pride before the 'ulama (scholars), nor by its help to quarrel with foolish people, nor through it try to overwhelm meetings, but he who does so, his destination is fire."* (Ibn Majah)

The purpose of seeking knowledge of the *deen* is solely to be in a better position to seek Allah's pleasure. Ignorance is not a valid excuse for neglecting *ibadah*, as we will be held accountable for the things which we could have found out but didn't.

The Qur'an

The starting point for acquiring religious knowledge is the word of Allah, the Qur'an. Being the 'Manufacturer's Manual' it contains all we need to know about how to conduct our daily lives, so we need to make it a part of our everyday life and refer to it regularly for the answers to our problems.

That means we need to read it every day in the form that it was revealed to us, i.e., in Arabic. If you can't read Arabic, then you need to make it a priority to learn how to read the Qur'an. If you can read Arabic but cannot understand it, then you will need to supplement your reading of the Qur'an with a translation while you learn to understand the Qur'an in Arabic. Of course, there are many translations and explanations (*tafaseer*) of the Qur'an that you can refer to, to give you greater insight and knowledge as well as listening to teachers that have more knowledge than us.

Sometimes it seems as though it doesn't make any difference whether we read the Qur'an or not and I am reminded of an e-mail I was sent about a boy who told his grandfather that he wasn't able to remember much of the Qur'an when he read it so what was the point of reading it? The grandfather told him to fetch him some water in his coal basket. So the boy went to fetch his grandfather some water in the coal basket. But, of course, by the time the little boy returned, all the water had run out of the basket and the basket was empty. The boy went three times to fetch water in the basket but each time he returned with an empty basket. Finally the boy gave up and told his grandfather that it was a useless exercise. The grandfather told the boy to look down at his basket. The basket that was black and dirty inside and outside from carrying coal, was now sparklingly clean. So even if we think that we cannot remember much of what we have read, we should never underestimate the effect that it has on our heart.

The Last Sermon

I have chosen to include the Last Sermon delivered by Prophet Muhammad ﷺ as it really touched me the first time I read it. There are many lessons we can learn from such a short speech that was delivered on 9th Dhul Hijjah10AH in the Uranah Valley of Mount Arafat.

> *"O People, lend me an attentive ear, for I don't know whether, after this year, I shall ever be amongst you again. Therefore listen to what I am saying to you carefully and take these words to those who could not be present here today.*
>
> *O People, just as you regard this month, this day, this city as sacred, so regard the life and property of every Muslim as a sacred trust. Return the goods entrusted to you to their rightful owners. Hurt no one so that no one may hurt you. Remember that you will indeed meet your Lord, and that He will indeed reckon your deeds. Allah has forbidden you to take usury (interest), therefore all interest obligation shall henceforth be waived...*
>
> *Beware of Shaytan, for your safety of your religion. He has lost all hope that he will ever be able to lead you astray in big things, so beware of following him in small things.*

O People, it is true that you have certain rights with regard to your women, but they also have rights over you. If they abide by your right then to them belongs the right to be fed and clothed in kindness. Do treat your women well and be kind to them for they are your partners and committed helpers. And it is your right that they do not make friends with any one of whom you do not approve, as well as never to commit adultery.

O People, listen to me in earnest, worship Allah, say your five daily prayers (salah), fast during the month of Ramadan, and give your wealth in Zakah. Perform Hajj if you can afford to. You know that every Muslim is the brother of another Muslim. You are all equal. Nobody has superiority over another except by piety and good action.

Remember, one day you will appear before Allah and answer for your deeds. So beware, do not astray from the path of righteousness after I am gone.

O People, no prophet or apostle will come after me and no new faith will be born. Reason well, therefore, O People, and understand my words which I convey to you. I leave behind me two things, the Qur'an and my example, the Sunnah and if you follow these you will never go astray.

All those who listen to me shall pass on my words to others and those to others again; and may the last ones understand my words better than those who listen to me directly. Be my witness, O Allah, that I have conveyed your message to your people."

There are many things we can take from this concise speech but I would like to highlight just a few things that may be relevant:

» We don't know when we are going to die

Even the Prophet ﷺ did not know the time of his death when he said, "I don't know whether, after this year, I shall ever be amongst you again." If the greatest person ever to live and the one most beloved by Allah did not know the time of his death then how can we be so arrogant and live our lives in a way that suggests that we are going to be here for many years to come?

» Responsibility to other Muslims

As Muslims we are instructed to regard the life and property of every Muslim as a sacred trust. We are told to return the goods entrusted to us to their rightful owners. This is such a minor command but how many of us borrow a small item from a friend for a week or two but end up holding onto it for months if not years?

» Don't Hurt Anyone

We are told not to hurt anyone so that no one may hurt us. Far too often we complain about how people treat us but we pay little attention as to how we treat the same people in return.

» Be Careful of Minor Sins

Many of us fall into the trap of knowingly committing what we may feel to be minor or small sins while we try and guard ourselves against the major sins. But we need to think why the Prophet Muhammad ﷺ warned us against following *Shaytan* in small things and not big things? This is because *Shaytan* uses the step-by-step approach that we looked at earlier. He fools us into thinking that committing small sins does not matter, but these small sins gradually erode away at our *iman*, like the dripping of water on a stone, to the point where we end up committing

Guidance and Learning

major sins without thinking twice about them. A sin is a sin and no sin should be taken lightly.

You people do (bad) deeds (commit sins) which seem in your eyes as tiny (minute) than hair while we used to consider those (very deeds) during the lifetime of the Prophet as destructive sins. (Anas ibn Malik)

Each time we commit a sin, it leaves a black spot on our heart. Our *iman* and consciousness of Allah (*taqwa*) are lowered slightly. This makes it that bit easier to commit the next sin which in turn leaves another black spot on the heart. If the sins are ignored, neither repented for nor erased by good deeds then the heart becomes covered in black. Allah puts a seal on it and the door of guidance is shut.

» *Treat Women Well*
Prophet Muhammad ﷺ is specifically instructing men to treat women well as they have been referred to as partners and helpers of men. He did not on this occasion stress to the women to treat their men well but instructed the men to treat the women well showing the respect and honour Allah has given to women for just being women and nothing else.

» *Equality*
Islam is a religion that abhors racism, ethnicism, tribalism, and its newer version, nationalism. Differences of language, colour, cuisine and accent were meant to add flavour to life, not to be used to ridicule or fight each other. We are told here that we are all equal but there is an exception. Superiority over another human being is not obtained because of gender, nationality, 'caste' or colour. We are who we are because of our good actions and level of piety.

Wouldn't it be great if your lecturers told you exactly what would be on this year's exam paper? Well the Prophet Muhammad ﷺ told us exactly how we can keep on the Straight Path – by following the Qur'an and his example, the *Sunnah*. Sounds pretty straightforward enough to me!

Your Bank Balance

When you start university, you will most probably find yourself living away from home for the first time in your life. This means that there will be added responsibilities to take care of in addition to studies, such as shopping, cooking, paying the rent on time and so on. In order to do all of those things, you will need to manage your finances and balance how much you earn (or receive) against how much you spend. Most universities have banks on campus and you need to talk to your branch to find out what facilities they offer to students. You need to check your statements regularly so you know what is entering and leaving your account and how healthy your balance is looking.

Whatever your specific financial arrangements, there is one thing to make clear at the start – interest is *haram*. That means that we cannot take interest and we should not pay it either, whatever the sums of money involved. Allah has made this clear in the Qur'an and the Prophet Muhammad ﷺ re-iterated this in the Last Sermon.

You who have iman! Do not feed on riba, multiplied and then re-multiplied. Have taqwa of Allah so that hopefully you will be successful. (Surah Ali-Imran 3:130)

Also, as an adult Muslim, you may be liable to pay *Zakah*, if you fulfil the criteria for doing so. You need to talk to a scholar to find out exactly what these are and how much you owe. But don't automatically think that just because you are a student, you don't have to pay *Zakah*.

The other account we need to regularly keep checking is our account of good and bad deeds. This is the account that will be examined on the Day of Judgement and we need to make sure that we have enough in our scale of good deeds to save us from the punishment of Hellfire. Unlike our bank accounts, it is far easier to maintain a healthy balance of good deeds as Ibn Abbas narrated that the Prophet ﷺ said:

> *"Allah records good and bad deeds in this way: If anyone intends to do a good deed, but does not do it, Allah still records it with Him as one full good deed. If he intends a good deed and then carries it out, Allah records it with Him as ten to seven hundred times in reward or even increases it many times more. If anyone intends to do a bad deed but does not actually do it, Allah records it with Him as one full good deed. If he intends to do a bad deed and does it, Allah records it with Him as only one bad deed."* (Bukhari)

The scales are so heavily tipped in our favour that if we think about doing something bad but don't actually do it, then we actually get rewarded for it! This shows us that Allah's love for us and His desire to see us succeed is deeper and vaster than anything we can imagine. This should be great encouragement for us to do good.

What's Your Legacy?

Most of us at some time or another have been in exams where we wished we were given more time to finish the questions, but unfortunately once the invigilators said stop, we had to stop.

However, in the exam of this life, it is not the same. Allah in His infinite mercy has informed us of ways we can continue to receive good deeds and rewards after our exam has ended and we have died! This is also known as *Sadaqah Jariya*. Abu Huraira ﷺ narrated that the Prophet ﷺ said:

"Verily, what reaches the mu'min of his good works and good acts, after his death, is the knowledge (benefitted from)... and a righteous child which he has left (behind him), or a book which he has given to inherit, or a place of worship which he has built, or a house for the homeless which he has built, or a canal which he has caused to be dug, or an act of charity which he has done out of his wealth while in his health and life. (The good effects thereof) reach him (even) after his death." (Tirmidhi, Bayhaqi and Ibn Majah)

So if we work to carry out some of these long-term projects, not only will we be helping people after our death, we will also be watching our balance of good deeds increase without having to do anything.

Chapter 4

The Importance of Time Management

Time Flies

One piece of advice I am sure that you will keep being given is that 'time flies'. Your lecturers and tutors will tell you how to manage your time effectively as it will go so quickly you won't realise. When you are sitting in the lecture theatre on the first day of your (typically) three year course, it seems that you have so much time ahead of you and what your lecturer is saying makes no sense at all. At the beginning of my five year stint at university, I remember feeling like that was an eternity, so I might as well take it easy at the start.

Well take it from me, you will quickly learn that there is never enough time in the day to attend your lectures, do the worksheets, have a life and keep yourself sane! The number of hours in the day is the same for everyone, so how come some people manage to get so much more done than others? The answer is time management.

To start with you need a diary that you can use to record your obligations. But time management is more than just keeping a diary. It requires you to identify the tasks you need to do, how important and/

or urgent they are and to make a decision about how much time you want to allocate to each task. This is true for each and every task from major pieces of coursework to chatting to friends on the phone and will help you use your time much more effectively. As a student, there are some basic principles of time management that you can apply.

» *Identify your best time for studying:*
Everyone has a time of day when they are more focused and alert and it is best to use this time for tasks that need more concentration, such as studying. Are you a 'morning person' or an 'evening person'? Use your 'best' times to study and allocate more menial tasks such as the laundry and shopping to times when you are not so mentally alert.

» *Get the difficult tasks out of the way first:*
If you have three assignments to do, don't automatically start with the easiest. When you are fresh, you can process information more quickly and save time as a result. When you are mentally tired, the same tasks can take so much longer. Also if you get the difficult or tedious tasks out of the way first, you will feel better for the rest of the day.

» *Study in shorter time blocks with short breaks between:*
Your mind cannot stay focused on one thing for hours at a time so ensure that you work in blocks of no more than one hour with a ten minute break in between. That ten minute break should not be used to check your e-mail but rather to get up and stretch your legs and have a change of scenery. This keeps you from getting fatigued and wasting time by being unproductive.

» *Make sure the surroundings are conducive to studying:*
Before you sit down to do a task, make sure that you have everything that you need to hand. This will save you from getting up and wasting time in looking for something.

» *Factor rest and relaxation into your schedule:*
University is not just about studying twenty-four-seven. In order to get the best out of your time here, you need to balance study with all the other facilities that university life has to offer.

» *Eat and sleep properly:*
If you don't look after yourself and take care of your basic needs then you cannot expect your mind and body to perform at their best. Schedule in a full night's sleep (waking up for *Fajr*, of course!) every night. An all-nighter should be the exception and not the norm. Also make sure you leave yourself time to cook and eat nutritious food. Takeaways and fast food are not the ideal fuel for your body.

» *Combine activities:*
If, for example, you are going down to the laundrette and have to spend an hour there while your clothes are washing and drying, then you might consider taking a book or your notes with you to read. This way, you get two activities done in one time slot.

» *Don't leave things to the last minute:*
Don't fall into the trap of thinking you have plenty of time to do something so you will leave it till later. If you have been given an assignment to complete in one week, then that is because you need a week to complete it. If you leave it till the night before, then you will not be able to do your best. Similarly, you will receive your exam timetable well in advance so start revising then. It will save you a great deal of stress!

Time in Islam

Time is honoured and precious in Islam. Even Allah has sworn by it:

By time. (Surah Al-'Asr 103:1)

But, we humans tend to underestimate the power of time and even to misunderstand it. We seem to think that we have much time ahead of us and we dream of a lifetime starting with a happy and carefree childhood, an exciting and even more carefree adolescent period, a meaningful period in our adulthood where we enjoy our work and get married and become parents before we reach old age when we retire and take it easy before we die. We would all like to believe and hope that we experience all of these stages in our life. Some of us even celebrate getting older by having parties and cutting cakes, but the scholars warn us:

> *Son of Adam! You are nothing but a number of days, whenever each day passes then part of you has gone.* (Al-Hasan Al-Basri)

We need to remember that our lifetime has been preordained, cannot be altered and is known to no one but Allah. This was well illustrated when once Prophet Muhammad ﷺ overheard his wife, Umm Habiba ﵂, making *du'a* to Allah for the long life of her father, Abu Sufyan, her brother, Mu'awiya, and Muhammad ﷺ for their long lives amongst other things. When she finished the *du'a*, Prophet Muhammad ﷺ said to her that it would have been better if she had asked Allah to spare them from the punishment of the grave and the punishment of Hellfire instead of their long lives, because the length of everyone's life is a term that is preordained and cannot be changed.

Luqman's Advice to his Son

If one subject of your course was to carry greater marks in the final exam than another, you would naturally spend more time studying it.

Luqman was a wise man mentioned in the Qur'an and one of the many pieces of advice he gave his son was to "Serve this world according to the time you are going to spend in it, and work for the *akhirah* according to the time you are going to spend in it."

We can hope to spend no more than one hundred years in this world against the eternity that we will spend in the Hereafter. So the ratio of time in this world to the time in the Hereafter is 100: infinity. This effectively means that we should be spending all our time preparing for the Hereafter and this leaves us no time at all to be worrying about the affairs of this world.

Hasan Al-Basri said about the righteous salaf, "I saw those people and how they were more careful about their time than about their money." (Al-Hasan Al-Basri)

Procrastination

Have you ever put your most important tasks off until later and then later and later, while you busied yourself with activities that were not so important? Did you hope that you would have more time and be in a better mood later to start the task and do it properly?

The essence of procrastination is very well reflected in this quote by Bernard Meltzer:

What is Procrastination? Procrastination is avoiding doing things that need to be done or leaving things undone for as long as possible.

"Hard work is often the easy work you did not do at the proper time." Don't worry - this happens with all of us time after time and not just at university!

But the most effective change you can make in your life is to recognise why you procrastinate and then deal with those reasons before this habit steals your opportunities and damages your career. If that sounds dramatic, that's because it's true. You can have the best mind in the world and yet you will fail if you don't get things done. Some of the reasons we procrastinate can be:

» Lack of clear goals
» Waiting for the right mood
» Waiting for the right time
» Laziness
» Underestimating the time required to complete the tasks
» Not understanding what is required to complete the task
» Fear of failure
» Underestimating the importance of the task

Put all these causes together and what happens? You do nothing! Whether it's a piece of coursework that you end up leaving to the night before the submission date or the exam that you try to revise for on the morning of the exam. If you are unclear about what you need to do then you should speak to your lecturer sooner rather than later and get help. If you need motivation then turn to one of your 'Smart' friends to pull you out of your lazy mood and get on with the work. But simply doing nothing should not be an option.

In fact, the same causes of procrastination are the reasons that some Muslims give for not doing their *salah*. How many people do you know that say, "We know we should pray and we will do it one day, insha'Allah."

Do not sit idle, for indeed death is seeking you. (Al-Hasan Al-Basri)

If we do a bit of soul-searching and are perfectly honest, then we have all used these sorts of excuses at one time or other in our lives. But if you are still procrastinating about important matters of the *deen*, then ask yourself, when will be the right time or the right place? What am I waiting for? If it's 'Divine Inspiration' or a 'Sign' from Allah, then let this book be exactly that and start from today!

Allah did not order the believing men and women (that's you and me) to pray when WE feel like it or when WE feel the time is right. We have the goal, we have been given the times in the day that we must pray and mood or no mood, that's what we have to do.

Performing *Hajj* is another obligation which unfortunately many people overlook as something they will do when they get older. In fact, I remember my father advising me to do *Hajj* in my youth as he found it physically demanding. This is a great illustration of how we make something hard work simply by not doing it at its proper time.

To eliminate the causes of procrastination, we should identify what we need to do and why and then just get on and do it! It's as simple as that.

Making Time for Salah

University life can be pretty hectic with all the lectures, seminars, presentations, private study time, social activities, work and family commitments. Amongst all these list of 'things to do', unfortunately sometimes *salah* gets neglected. Some people just don't pray at all, while others don't give it the importance it deserves. Why is that?

I think that most people will fall into two main groups. The first group just don't realise the benefits of prayer and completely underestimate its importance in their life. They have a very relaxed attitude to time and live in the (false!) hope that there is plenty of time to start praying once they get older. They think their youth is a time to enjoy themselves and *salah* will just get in the way of that. These people rarely perform their *salah* (probably only *Jumu'ah* and *'Eid* prayers, if at all).

Then you have the second group who are a bit lazy about prayer. They'll get up and pray if the opportunity presents itself, for example, when they are at home and mum tells them to but they won't make an effort to establish their *salah* five times a day. These people always have an excuse:

» 'I don't have my *wudu.*'
» 'I don't have anything to cover my hair with.'
» 'I can't pray here, it's a public place and people will stare!'
» 'I don't have time right now.'

So let's address these issues, starting with the importance and the benefits of establishing the *salah*.

The Importance of Salah

Human beings are not robots and we don't just do exactly as we are told, without having some sort of motivation and understanding of why we need to do a task. That is true for everything from brushing your teeth to being at university.

Allah understands that this is a part of human nature and has therefore, not only provided us with details of the deeds that we must perform but He has also given us the reasons why we should do them and what will be the benefit. There are numerous references in the Qur'an and the *hadith* of the benefits and importance of *salah*. Just as students attend university for different reasons, so Allah has presented various reasons for praying so that each individual can find the reason that motivates them.

We have mentioned that our goal in life is the pleasure of Allah and entry into *Jannah*. *Salah* is the basic means to achieve this and neglecting the *salah* will incur the displeasure of Allah as He states:

> But after them there followed a posterity who missed prayers and followed after lusts. Soon then will they face destruction.
> (Surah Maryam 19:59)

On the Day of Judgement, the *salah* will be the first thing we are asked about our account of deeds.

The Importance of Time Management

The first of the actions of a person to be considered on the Day of Judgement is their salah. If it is accepted from them, the rest of their actions are considered; if not then none of the rest of their actions will be considered. (Muwatta al-Malik)

So it doesn't matter how much charity you give, how much voluntary work you do or how kind you are, these things are of no use without the foundation upon which all good deeds rest, which is the *salah*.

If we do not pray, it is a simple fact that we will be thrown into *Jahannum*, at least for a period of time to punish us. After this time, Allah may, in His mercy choose to take us out and grant us entry into *Jannah*. Now, you might think that that's alright – you get to *Jannah* eventually so it doesn't matter if you spend a little time in *Jahannum*. Think again! I would urge you read a detailed description of the horrors of *Jahannum* and I guarantee that when you have finished reading it, you will be doing your next *salah*!

The righteous salaf were as fearful of their good deeds being squandered, or not being accepted, as the present generation is certain that their neglect will be forgiven. (Al-Hasan Al-Basri)

But acts of worship are not just meaningless rituals that Allah has asked us to do for His pleasure alone. They are acts that benefit us as individuals as well as on a community level. When your parents want you to do well in your studies and go university, they are not just saying it for their pleasure. They want the best for you and the knowledge that they have left a good legacy to society as well as their pleasure in seeing you succeed. In the same way, it makes no difference to Allah's majesty or power whether you personally pray or not. The fact is that it is good for you. How?

The Benefits of Salah

The Prophet Muhammad ﷺ put it beautifully when he likened *salah* to a river in which a person bathes five times a day and asked his Companions whether any dirt would remain on their body. Those present answered that it would not (Bukhari, Muslim, Tirmidhi, Nasai). So *salah* is a means of cleansing your heart, of wiping away the minor sins that we invariably commit between prayers, of adding to the scale of good deeds so that the heart is as clean as the body would be if we bathed five times day.

Life has become rather stressful and people are now turning to ways of relaxing. Some people take up yoga, others meditate or just relax in a nice warm bubble bath. Well have you ever thought of *salah* as a de-stresser? If you do it properly, it provides a wonderful time out from the stresses of this world and the opportunity to connect with Allah, Who loves you more than your own parents do! In fact in a day filled with lectures and deadlines, *salah* is something you can look forward to to give you a break and a perspective on what is important.

Wudu

One barrier most people come across is not having *wudu*. It's the thought of doing *wudu* that deters a lot of people from praying and certainly was one of my mental blocks!

The pre-requisite to performing *salah* is to be in a state of purity. That means that your body and clothes should be free of any discharge from your body and that you take a full ritual bath (*ghusl*) upon becoming impure (after menstruation, sexual intercourse, nocturnal discharge). If you visit the toilet then you should clean yourself with water each time (*istanja*). While you should have a Muslim shower, jug or something similar at home to perform *istanja*, public toilets will obviously not have these facilities. So you need to be prepared and carry a large water bottle or something similar with you when you leave home. If you do not perform *istanja* then your *wudu* will not be valid and by extension, neither will your *salah*.

Performing *wudu* at home should not be a problem and you should try to leave home in state of *wudu*. At university your Islamic society prayer room should offer the facility to make *wudu*. However, if you are unable to get there or you don't have this facility then many people are embarrassed about performing *wudu* in a public WC where other people can see. I remember the first time I made *wudu* in the university toilets and believe me that was the quickest *wudu* I have ever done. I didn't want anyone to see me and start to think that I don't bathe at home and that I am having a mini bath in public! Washing our feet in the public toilet sinks can not only be embarrassing but you have to be something of a gymnast to get your feet and legs up there in the first place without toppling over! The thing to bear in mind is that you are doing *wudu* for the pleasure of Allah and so it really does not matter what anyone else thinks. You need to be careful that you do not use excessive water to perform your *wudu* and also that you do not leave wet puddles everywhere after you have finished that cause any inconvenience to anyone.

The other thing that people don't realise is that *wudu* is actually an act of worship in itself, not just a pre-requisite to *salah*. Doing *wudu* carries its own benefits and rewards as 'Uthman ☼ said that the Prophet ☼ said:

> *"Whoever makes wudu and makes it well, his sins come out from his body, even coming out from under his nails."* (Muslim)

Not only are we physically cleansed from the dust and grime of the day, but also spiritually cleansed – and that is before we have even done our *salah*!

Making Salah Easy

It makes it easier to perform *salah* if you have everything prepared beforehand and have pre-empted all the possible excuses you could make so that *Shaytan* can't talk you out of praying!

Now that you have done *wudu*, you need to be dressed appropriately. Guys should make sure that at least the area between the navel and the knees are covered in loose clothing. Girls should make sure that no part of the body can be seen except for the face and hands. If you do not normally wear a *hijab* or your clothes are not appropriate, then carry a covering with you at all times, so that does not stop you from praying.

Also carry a light prayer mat with you (it need only be a small clean square of cloth) and a small compass, so that you always have something clean to pray on and can find out the *qiblah*.

Now you have everything you need to pray, the last question is where do you pray if you cannot get to a *masjid* or prayer room? Well that's the simplest thing. Anywhere! That's right, you can pray anywhere on land or sea that is clean of impurity. You see, Allah tells us the whole world is a *masjid*, so we don't have to be in a special place to remember Allah. Hudaifa ﷺ reported that the Messenger of Allah ﷺ said:

> *"We have been made to excel (other) people in three (things): Our rows have been made like the rows of the angels and the whole earth has been made a mosque for us, and its dust has been made a purifier for us in case water is not available."*
> (Muslim)

The Prophet ﷺ and his Companions were commanded to pray in the middle of battles, while fighting was going on all around them! One group of *Sahabah* would pray while the other would guard them and then they would swap duties. If prayer was not excused for the Prophet ﷺ in that extreme situation of life and death, then what excuse do we have for not praying? So whether we are in the middle of a cricket match, out in the park, on holiday skiing or in the middle of the ocean – we have to pray.

We have to make time in the day to pray. After all we are busy people, but we all find the time to do the things that we think are important. We make time to socialise, or to watch that film or surf the net. So we need to make time to fulfil this fundamental obligation that has so many benefits and rewards for us.

In any case, if you neglect your prayer, then what right do you have to ask Allah for anything, to help you in your exams, to answer your *du'a*? If you make the excuse that you do not have time for Allah, then you cannot expect that He should make time for you. The Prophet ﷺ said,

> *"If someone wants to know what position he enjoys in the eyes of Allah, he has only to look at what place he gives to Allah (in his heart and life)."* (Hakim)

Got Time to Kill?

If we were to be told by our doctor that we only had days to live, would we still be looking to kill time or would we frantically try to cram in as many good deeds as possible before our time was up?

The fact is, that we don't need a doctor to tell us that our time is running out and that from the moment we are born, the timer is counting down the days until our eventual death. We must therefore utilise our time wisely and make the most of it while we still have the opportunity. Ibn Abbas ﷺ narrated that the Messenger of Allah ﷺ said:

> *"There are two blessings which many people lose: health and free time for doing good."* (Bukhari)

Unfortunately too many of us, including myself, waste this priceless commodity far too often and at times without even realising it. How many times have you heard or even used the phrase 'I'm killing time'? Just as in an exam we don't have time to kill, we really don't have enough time to kill in our lives.

A *mu'min*'s work is never done. If we are sitting a three hour exam and are finished in two and a half hours, we are advised to go over our work and look to correct any mistakes and to make sure we have not missed anything. Also, if an exam has been designed for three hours, then it is meant to take around three hours to finish.

Our lifespan should likewise be fully utilised to make sure we have not left anything undone that we could have added to our scale of good deeds with. This is the only chance we get; there will be no exams after this, only results. Therefore, we have to give this one exam our best shot.

It is a most amazing thing that you should continue to be unmindful, chasing after vain desires, wasting your time in disregard of this most important matter, for you are being driven at a fierce pace (towards death) day and night, hour by hour, like the blink of an eye. (Imam Ahmad ibn Hanbal)

Tips on Making Use of 'Dead Time'

I feel it is important to re-emphasise here the concept of worship in Islam. We are not angels who do no wrong nor are we robots who do what they are programmed to do. We are humans and we are not perfect. We need rest, we need to interact and socialise with others, and we need to eat, drink, sleep, get married and have children and a whole lot more.

All these things can be acts of worship if we remember our Creator in doing them and do them according to His guidance. Putting all these activities aside, we still have a lot of 'dead' time in our lives which could be put to better use.

For example, personally I spend up to one hour in my car every day commuting. Like most people, I always used to listen to music or the radio. Then one day a friend of mine gave me a set of audio lectures on Islam. Now I have always struggled to find the time to read so this was ideal for me. Not only have I learnt a great deal but I also feel energised after being in the company of inspiring speakers.

The Importance of Time Management

It doesn't matter if you only have ten minutes at a time or whether you listen to a speaker or the recitation of the Qur'an. All these little chunks of time will add up fast. Just think of all the knowledge you can gain or *surah*s you can memorise in just a few months with very little effort on your part. Unfortunately having been brought up listening to Bollywood songs and by listening to them over and over again I became a '*hafiz*' of many complete songs without even trying to do so. But, *alhamdulillah*, since I started listening to the Qur'an instead of music in my car, I ended up memorising a number of *surah*s of the Qur'an, quite effortlessly!

Finding Time to do Dhikr *of Allah*

We all get stuck in the occasional queue at times whether in the bank or the post office, and we all walk to and from the station or the shops and so on. These are perfect opportunities to do *dhikr* as this is pretty much dead time where you can't do much else.

Dhikr is simply remembering Allah and can be done quite easily amongst our mundane daily activities. In fact it is the easiest form of worship as it does not require us to be in a state of *wudu* and it can take different forms.

The most common forms of *dhikr* are reciting *SubhanAllah*, *Alhamdulillah* and *Allahu Akbar* or many other words and phrases that glorify Allah; reciting His Names or reciting any portion of the Qur'an that you have memorised. In fact, anything that reminds you of Allah is *dhikr*.

So what is the point of *dhikr*? Well first of all, it brings peace to our hearts:

> *...Without doubt in the remembrance of Allah do hearts find satisfaction.* (Surah Ar-Ra'd 13:28)

Most people are searching for the meaning of life or for peace of mind and contentment. Well, we Muslims have the prescription right here and it is very simple!

There is no doubt that the heart becomes covered with rust, just as metal dishes - silver, and their like - become rusty. So the rust of the heart is polished with dhikr, for dhikr polishes the heart until it becomes like a shiny mirror. However, when dhikr is abandoned, the rust returns; and when it commences then the heart again begins to be cleansed. Thus the heart becoming rusty is due to two matters: sins and ahafah (neglecting remembrance of Allah). Likewise, it is cleansed and polished by two things: istighfar and dhikr. (Ibn Qayyim Al-Jawziyyah)

If our hearts and tongues are always engaged in the remembrance of Allah, it is harder for us to think about doing something bad or to backbite or gossip, so *dhikr* protects us as well as nourishing our souls. It helps us focus on Allah and diverts our attention from our mundane problems and difficulties. In fact, it is more than beneficial for us; we need to do *dhikr* for our well-being.

> *Dhikr is to the heart as water is to a fish; see what happens to a fish when it is taken out of water.* (Ibn Taymiyyah)

Juggling Obligations and Responsibilities

At every stage of our lives, but more so as we get older, we have obligations and responsibilities to Allah, to our families and to the people around us. As well as satisfying everyone, we have to work, socialise a little and make time for *ibadah* and rest. Sometimes in the attempt to keep everyone happy, there are times when we stretch ourselves and over commit only to find that we cannot fulfil our commitments. Anas ﷺ narrated that the Messenger of Allah ﷺ said:

> *"He has (really) no faith who fulfils not his trust, and he has (really) no religion who fulfils not his promise."* (Ahmad)

It is important not to make promises that we cannot keep and to keep all those promises that we do make. We should always try and keep our word, however trivial it may seem. If we say that we will meet with a friend at 1pm, that means that we should be true to our word and be punctual. If we say that we will call someone, then we should do so promptly.

It may seem that these are small matters not worth mentioning but just as one drop of urine spoils a whole jug of water, one seemingly insignificant lie or broken promise can taint our whole *iman*. One minute means sixty seconds everywhere, no more. Make a habit of under-committing rather than over-committing.

Dealing with Stress

There are bound to be times at university when you feel overwhelmed with stress. It is a big life change and there are many things to get to grips with: leaving home, being in a completely different environment, managing your own life independently, juggling study and social life. Towards the end of the course, there is the added pressure of doing well in your exams, perhaps parental pressure and the need to find a good job.

The first thing to remember is not to let the stress build up until you feel you can no longer cope. This is not good for either your physical or your mental health. There are usually two kinds of stress – the type that is somewhat created by our own doing and the other which we can do absolutely nothing about. You can minimise the first type of stress by:

» Stop procrastinating
» Get organised
» Clarify your priorities
» Manage your time
» Deal with paperwork promptly (that includes lecture notes, bills, bank statements and letters)

A lot of pre-exam stress or pre-deadline stress can be alleviated if you get things done in good time and pace yourself. It is also important to eat and sleep properly as I mentioned before, because your body and mind need to be in top condition if you want them to do all that you demand.

Secondly, you need to know that you have a support network of people that can help you. You should be able to talk to family, friends or student counsellors to help you see your problem in perspective and to work through it.

As Muslims, we also have another very powerful tool at our disposal and that is our faith. All too often, we see people turning to Allah when they are in trouble. But if you build up your knowledge and strengthen your *iman* during periods of comfort and ease, then you have a reserve of *iman* to draw upon when you face hardship or suffering.

One of the tenets of *iman* is belief in *qadar* (the Decree of Allah). However, we do not know what our destiny holds for us so we have to make our best efforts and leave it at that. Once we have made our best preparations and submitted our coursework or sat the exam, we should not stress ourselves, but leave the result in Allah's hands as He is the best planner of our affairs. This is a very comforting thought and should leave us content and tranquil rather than despairing and depressed. Abu Suhayb ibn Sinan ◈ narrated that the Prophet ◈ said:

> *"How amazing is the case of the believer; there is good for him in everything, and this characteristic is exclusively for him alone. If he experiences something pleasant, he is thankful, and that is good for him; and if he comes across some difficulty, he is patient, and that is good for him."* (Muslim)

Of course, it is human nature to want a life of ease and comfort, but to expect that is not in keeping with a Muslim's view of this world.

The Importance of Time Management

Whoever wants to have everlasting peace and well-being with no affliction does not understand the meaning of Allah's commandments, nor does he perceive the meaning of submission to Allah. Every soul (either believing or disbelieving) shall inevitably taste suffering in this world, for this life is based on hardships. Man lives between comfort and suffering. (Imam ibn Al-Jawzee)

The test is about our performance in given circumstances, not about how good or bad our circumstances are. We should bear any suffering with patience and steadfastness and there is a great reward for that:

...Those who patiently persevere will truly receive a reward without measure. (Surah Az-Zumar 39:10)

Whatever hardships, tests, trials and sufferings we endure during our servitude to Him are all part of His plan for our ultimate success. Enduring them with patience, without complaint, and without being disheartened, is part of our job as His slaves.

Real success is attaining the pleasure of Allah, not results in this world. Whatever comes our way, we must continue on our course of life steadfastly and be grateful for all that we have. If we truly trust in Allah and depend on Him alone, then we will not live with regrets about the past nor will we have any fear for the future, but just do what is within our control and leave what is not in the Most Capable hands of Allah.

Whosoever follows My guidance, on them shall be no fear, nor shall they grieve. (Surah Al-Baqarah 2:38)

Chapter 5

Final Exams

At the end of your course, you will most probably have final exams that thoroughly test you on all aspects of your study. How you perform in these exams over the course of a few weeks will determine what class of degree you obtain and have an impact on the job that you get. All those years of study and sacrifice need to show in these exam papers, so it is natural that you will feel under pressure. But how do you use that pressure to your advantage and perform to your best at this stressful time?

Preparing For Exams

There is absolutely no substitute for regular and steady preparation throughout the entire duration of your course. If you have attended all your lectures and tutorials, made notes and filed them in order, completed the worksheets and kept revisiting your work at the end of each term, then you are at a great advantage. Your brain has absorbed the information that you have given it over a period of time and it has become embedded in your mind. There is no last minute panicking and cramming needed. Your exam preparation should consist of practising problems under timed conditions and looking at past exam papers.

If you haven't been quite so organised then stop procrastinating and start revising! First of all, you need to make sure that your notes are complete and in order. Then you simply need to sit down, stop finding other things to do and force yourself to revise. Set yourself small targets to begin with (for example, I will do three problems from the end of chapter 1 under timed conditions). Build up your confidence and your tolerance for working and soon you will be making serious progress. If you are still finding it difficult to get down to work, then re-visit the procrastination section and address the causes of your procrastination. Your future depends on it!

It can be overwhelming when you have years of study to process to know where to start. Break down your course into manageable chunks and make a timetable that allocates time to all of these chunks. Once you have developed a routine and allocated time to all your subjects then stick to it. Do your least favourite subject or the one you find most difficult earlier in the day to get it out of the way. Do not underestimate the important of relaxing. You should aim to come away from your desk after one hour of study for about ten minutes. You need to give yourself a complete break and have something to look forward to every day. This can be a relaxing bath, a workout in the gym or anything that takes your mind off exams.

It is not just a question of putting in the hours, you need to develop an effective revision technique and that does not entail lying in bed reading a textbook. After ten minutes your eyes will glaze over and you will end up falling asleep. Like lectures, revision needs to have active input from you to make it enjoyable and to engage your brain so that it remembers more. Some things you can do are:

» Revise in a group with other students – but do be careful that you don't get distracted
» Write up chapter summaries
» Draw diagrams
» Make posters
» Do textbook questions, worksheets and past exam papers

Again, you need to find what works best for you. If you have perfected your revision technique in the earlier years you will not need to spend time doing this in the later years.

While you need all the knowledge that you have gained to be fresh in your mind for the exam, don't be fooled into thinking that you will achieve this by leaving your revision till the last minute. Your brain will not have had time to process all the information so it will just leave you feeling muddled and anxious. If you have been revising in advance, then you can always revisit your work nearer the time to keep it fresh in your mind. However tempting it is to cram until the last minute, do make the time to get a good night's sleep the night before an exam and a good nutritious breakfast in the morning. And lastly, it might sound obvious but check your exam timetable for the correct time and place of your exam and make sure that you arrive well before it begins.

Death

You realise just how much is riding on your exam results, and so you do your best to get good marks because you know this will open the door to good job prospects and all the advantages that come with that. Even the most 'Chilled Out' student can be found with their head in a book the night before an exam!

The good thing about final exams is that you know that they will always come at the end of your course and you know when that is. The thing about life is that we don't know when ours will end. We can certainly delude ourselves into thinking that we will see our old age, but you just have to look at the obituary columns in the papers to see that people can die at any time. There are fatal accidents, but somehow we think that will never happen to us. One minute we could be travelling happily in our cars on the motorway and before we know it, a lorry has gone across the carriageway and hit the car head on. If both vehicles are travelling at an average speed of 70 mph, that's a combined collision at 140 mph. You would be dead in seconds…

A young, healthy professional footballer is one of the last people that you would expect to die due to health problems at an early age. Miklos Feher was a 25 year-old footballer. In a live televised football match, he was caught on camera smiling before he bent down to take a deep breath. He collapsed and died there and then leaving the players, the fans in the stadium and the TV audience in utter shock and disbelief. No matter what the post-mortem examination revealed the cause of death to be, the simple fact is that this young man's time on this earth was finished and Allah asked the Angel of Death to take his soul.

Talking about death makes us uncomfortable and one of the reasons we don't think about our death is because it simply frightens us. We don't know what to expect. The thought of swapping the comfort of our beds for the grave sends a shiver down our spine so we ignore it as if it is never going to happen.

To an Umayyad caliph's question, "Why do we fear death?", Ibn Hazm replied, "Because we hate to go from what we have built to what we have destroyed." We spend all our time, efforts and money in acquiring houses that are filled with the most beautiful possessions, clothes, cars, businesses and indeed it shows. Because we have invested so much of ourselves in this *dunya*, then our heart gets involved here and does not want to leave. When we try to imagine our property in the *akhirah* we don't see anything, or at best, we are uncertain. Thus, we don't feel comfortable about going there. But our death will bring an end to this life and will take us to the life of that uncertain place anyway so it's not a question of choice; it's facing the fact that it's going to happen and best preparing for it.

Whoever enters his grave without any provisions is like the one who mounts the sea without a ship. (Abu Bakr As-Siddiq ﷺ)

Preparing for the Akhirah

We might not know when we will die and have our preparation time cut short, but we do know what questions we will be asked on the Day of the Final Exam, the Day of Judgement.

The *salah* is the first thing that we will be asked about on the Day on Judgement. If we can pass this question, then all of our deeds will be judged in the same way. So in order to get through the first part of our exam, we need to ensure that our *salah* is in order. How do we do that? We need to have completed the *fard* component of our *salah* as well as the *sunnah* components regularly and on time. A'ishah ﷺ narrated that the Messenger of Allah ﷺ said:

> *"Whoever is regular with twelve rak'at of Sunnah (prayer), Allah will build a house for him in Paradise: four rak'at before Zuhr, two rak'at after it, two rak'at after Maghrib, two rak'at after Isha, and two rak'at before Fajr."* (Tirmidhi)

Offering *nafl* prayers will get you extra brownie points and cover you if you there have been gaps in performing the *sunnah* and *fard*. Then Allah will look at our other deeds (such as fasting) in the same way, first the *fard* then the *sunnah* and finally the *nafl*.

Sahl ibn Sa'd ﷺ reported that the Prophet ﷺ said:

> *"Jannah has eight gates and one of them is called Ar-Rayyan, through will none will enter except those who observe fasting."* (Bukhari)

So we learn from this *hadith* that certain deeds will provide us with the key to the gates of *Jannah*. It makes sense then that we should use the keys. How else will we be able to enter?!

Another way to prepare for the *akhirah* is to invest in it. Just as we all look out for 'Investment Opportunities' in this life where we hope to put in a little and gain a lot, we need to identify these opportunities and investments where we can build up an empire for ourselves in the *akhirah* and so look forward to actually getting there! There are many small acts that will pay huge dividends on a minimal investment and the following *hadith* gives just one example. Sa'd ibn Abi Waqqas ﷺ reported:

> *"We were with Allah's Messenger ﷺ when he asked, 'Will any of you have the capacity of performing one thousand good deeds daily?' One of those who were attending his company asked, 'How can one thousand virtuous acts be performed in a day?' He replied, 'If one glorifies Allah one hundred times, one thousand good deeds will be recorded for him or one thousand sins will be blotted out from his record.'"* (Muslim)

Most of us work very hard all day for a basic wage and even the high earners amongst us have to earn it through putting in long hours. How long does it take for us to say *'Subhan Allah'* a hundred times and just look at the reward for it? That sounds like a pretty good investment to me!

As we have seen before, worship in Islam is not just about praying and fasting. Everything we do, day in day out can be accruing rewards for us on the Day of Judgement – all we have to do is acknowledge Allah in doing them and do them for His pleasure. That could be: removing a stone from the road so that it does not harm someone, giving someone a glass of water, paying attention to a small child, giving of your time to the elderly, sharing a skill that you have, helping with the housework and the list is endless. In fact you'll find that there are literally hundreds of opportunities to earn Allah's pleasure every day. Each kindness, however insignificant you think it is, will count in your favour on the Day of Judgement, if done with sincerity.

If you don't find sweetness and joy in the deed you perform, then doubt its sincerity, for Allah is Shakur (Most Appreciative and Rewarding). (Ibn Taymiyyah)

In the Exam Hall

This is crunch time! There is no going back from here. Almost everyone feels nervous before an exam and worries whether they have done enough revision, whether they will be able to answer the questions and suddenly thinks of something that they should have revised.

Instead of letting these thoughts crowd your mind and make you even more nervous, put a stop to them and focus on something else that relaxes you. This could be a phrase that you repeat to calm yourself down or a mental picture of a relaxing place. Avoid talking to other students at this time, you'll only get more nervous.

I used to get myself so worked up before exams that I would get nightmares. From my experience, I would recommend the following approach: find your seat in the exam room, take a deep breath in and out and begin in the name of Allah. Before you even put pen to paper, read through the whole script in its entirety once over, bearing in mind how many questions there are and how the marks are allocated. Usually you'll find one question that you are confident about. Start with that one and hopefully by then the butterflies in your stomach will have settled down a bit. If you find yourself spending too much time on one question, move onto the next one.

If you start to panic at any stage, then close your eyes and repeat your relaxing phrase or imagine your relaxing place, which should calm you down. But be careful that you don't spend too much time distracting yourself with thoughts of relaxing on a hammock in the Bahamas!

Remember that while nobody actually looks forward to exams you should look at these as an opportunity for you to show the examiners how much you know and understand. Without passing the exams you wouldn't be able to get the degree, which is the key to opening the door to potentially better job prospects.

Final Exams

What if I Fail an Exam?

If you fail, the first thing to expect is an earful from your parents! Naturally, all parents have a lot of expectations from their children and if you have come this far, then they will want to see you do well so if you don't then they will not be too pleased.

Seriously, though, if you have failed your end of year or end of course exams, it can be hard to see everything in perspective. There is of course, your disappointment, your family's disappointment and then having to explain to everyone who asks what you got, that you didn't quite make it.

Failing your exams is not the end of the world. It's happened and there is nothing you can do about it, but how you deal with it is what actually matters. It's like falling off your bike when you were younger – you could either stay on the ground crying or you could pick yourself up, dust yourself down and get back on the bike.

> *Do not detest the misfortunes that befall you, for what you detest may be the cause of your salvation and what you like may be the cause of your ruin.* (Al-Hasan Al-Basri)

So how do you come to terms with it? I believe the first and the most important factor is your mental toughness. If you can show resilience in the most difficult times then *insha'Allah* you will be destined for success. The change has to come from within, there has to be a sense of urgency in understanding the possible reasons of failure.

Discuss the situation with your tutor. Did you fail a couple of subjects, in which case you could probably re-sit your exams later in the summer and no-one would be any the wiser?

If you failed many subjects by a long way, then you have to sit down and decide what you want to do next. If the cause of your failure is simply that you did not work hard or underestimated the importance of your exams, then you know what you need to do and learn from your mistakes.

If, however, you are finding it difficult to manage even though you are putting in the effort, then you need to consider whether you are on the right course, at the right university and following the best career path for yourself.

You are at one of life's crossroads and while you might not like it, you have a choice about where you want to go next. You have the opportunity to go down a different route now and that is often harder the later you are in life. Take on board the advice of your tutor, lecturers, parents and family but it is ultimately your decision as you are the one who has to do this.

And remember that having a degree is not a prerequisite to success, so keep things in perspective!

The planning of The Almighty (Allah) is better for you than your own planning, and He could deprive you from what you ask to test your patience. So let Him see from you a determined patience and you will soon see from Him what will give you joy. And when you have cleaned the paths of answering (of supplication) from the stains of sin and were patient about what He has chosen for you, then everything that happens to you is better for you whether you were given or deprived of what you have requested. (Imam ibn Al-Jawzee)

The Next Stage

Death is inevitable to us all. Facing the reality of death, particularly one's own mortality, can create feelings of fear and anxiety. Death is also viewed by everyone as a tragedy. But is it really a tragedy?

As Muslims, we believe that death is not the end but just the next stage in our soul's journey. It simply marks the stage where the body and soul are separated. If you perceive death to be the end, then it can instill a lot of fear and anxiety while if you just think of it as a transitional phase, it can bring feelings of calm, satisfaction and hope. It's the phase you have to pass through so that you can get to where you want to be – which is *Jannah*.

Most of us are afraid of things we don't understand or know much about and the biggest of these unknowns is death. But we have been given plenty of information about death, life in the grave, the Day of Judgement and detailed descriptions of *Jannah* and *Jahannum* in the Qur'an and *hadith*, so that we can get an idea of what is to come.

In the Qur'an, Allah tells us that:

> *Verily, those who say: "Our Lord is Allah (Alone)," and then they stand firm, on them the angels will descend (at the time of their death) (saying): "Fear not, nor grieve! But receive the glad tidings of Paradise which you have been promised!"*
> (Surah Fussilat 40:30)

From the *hadith*, 'Ubadah ibn as-Samit ﷺ narrated that the Prophet ﷺ said:

> *"Whoever loves to meet Allah should know that Allah loves to meet him." Someone said, "But we dislike death." The Prophet ﷺ explained, "It is not (as you think): When the time of a believer's death approaches, he receives the good news of Allah's being pleased with him and His blessings upon him, and at that time nothing is dearer to him than what is in front of him. He therefore loves the meeting with Allah, and Allah too loves meeting him. But when the time of an unbeliever's death approaches, he receives the evil news of Allah's torment and His punishment, whereupon nothing is more hateful to him. Thus he hates meeting with Allah and Allah, too, hates meeting him."* (Bukhari)

Now once the soul has departed from the body, the next stage begins which is called *Barzakh*. This is the state that the soul remains in between the *dunya* and the *akhirah*. This is a bit like the period between having sat your exam and results day; it's hugely nerve-wracking because there is nothing you can but wait to find out what marks you got!

Every student, however, has some idea of how they have done and whether they have passed or failed immediately after the exam. It's just a matter of seeing exactly what marks they have attained. This waiting period can be an easy time for those students who know that they have done well and they almost look forward to receiving their results. However, it can be a time of great anxiety for the students that know that they haven't done enough and they may be regretting all those times that they didn't study. But regrets are useless as you can never turn back the clock.

In the same way, the time in the grave can either be an easy one or a most difficult one depending on the level of preparation that a person did during their lifetime.

> *[Once, 'Uthman] stood by the side of a grave and wept so bitterly that his beard became wet with tears. It was said to him, "You do not weep over the discussion of Jannah and Jahannum, but you weep over the grave." Whereupon he reported the Messenger of Allah* ﷺ *as saying: "Verily the grave is the first step in the stages of the Hereafter; if someone finds salvation [at this stage], the succeeding stages become easy for him, and if someone does not find salvation in it, what follows is very hard upon him."* (Tirmidhi)

Once in the grave the dead man is visited by two fearsome angels, Munkar and Nakir, who question the soul about its religion, Allah and the Prophet Muhammad ﷺ. This is a very hard test but the believing slave of Allah is able to answer these questions correctly and with confidence. His good deeds, such as his prayer, his fasting, his recitation of the Qur'an, his charity, his patience and kindness to relations, are scattered around him and defend him from the severe questioning of the angels. At this point, his grave is made more spacious and pleasant for him with a window through which he can see his promised place in *Jannah*.

Conversely, if a person is unable to answer the questions, then the angels will beat him with iron bars and torture him, the unbeliever's grave closes in on him so much that it crushes his ribs and he has a window opening that shows him his place in *Jahannum*.

Judgement Day

All souls will remain in this state of *Barzakh* in their graves until the Angel Israfil blows the trumpet and all souls that have ever existed from the beginning until the end of time are resurrected on a vast plain.

> *On the Day (when the first blowing of the Trumpet is blown), the earth and the mountains will shake violently (and everybody will die), the second blowing of the Trumpet follows it (and everybody will be resurrected).* (Surah An-Naziat 79:6-7)

On that day, the sun will be brought overhead so that it is unbearably hot. People will be drenched in their sweat according to the amount of their sins. Some will be ankle deep in it; some will be in it up to their ears. The Day of Judgement will be 50,000 years in length and will seem like an eternity to the one who is unprepared but according to a *hadith* it will become shorter for the believer than the prayer he used to perform in this world (Ibn Hanbal). On that day there will no shade except for the seven categories of people who earn the shade of Allah that we mentioned in Chapter 2.

It will be a terrifying day when no one will help another:

> *What will convey to you what the Day of Judgement is? Again! What will convey to you what the Day of Judgement is? It is the Day when a self will have no power to help any other self in any way. The command that Day will be Allah's alone.* (Surah Al-Infitar 82:17-19)

The only things that can save us are the deeds that we did in this world. Our books of deeds will be put on the scales and we will await with trepidation as to whether the good deeds outweigh the bad. At this point there will be a person whose scale of good deeds is heavy but he will still go to Hell. Who is this unfortunate person?

The Prophet ﷺ said, "The bankrupt of my nation is he who comes forth on the Day of Judgement with salah, fasting and Zakah, but having insulted this man, and abused that man, and having consumed another's wealth, and shed another's blood and struck yet another. Each one of these shall be given a portion of his good works, and should these be exhausted before his obligation is discharged then he shall be assigned some of their sins, which will be heaped upon him. Then he shall be cast into hell." (Muslim)

This is the day of Allah's Perfect Justice. There is much injustice on the earth but on that day, it will all be put right, and each oppressed human being will receive justice from Allah against his oppressor. This book of deeds will contain each and every act, no matter how insignificant, that we will be in awe as to how detailed this account is:

Then shall anyone who has done an atom's weight of good see it! And anyone who has done an atom's worth of evil shall see it. (Surah Az-Zalzalah 99:7-8)

Then we are given our book of deeds, either in our right hand or in our left hand, according to whether we have been successful or not.

At this point everyone has to cross the bridge or *As-Sirat*. This stretches over Hell and is as sharp as a sword and thinner than a hair. Those who have a faultless book of good deeds will be able to cross the *Sirat* like the wind. Those that have an increasing number of bad deeds on their record will enter walking, crawling and even being snagged by the iron hooks that claw at them. Some will fall into the

Hellfire below while those that reach the other side are admitted into *Jannah, insha'Allah.*

Some people will enter *Jahannum* first and are punished according to the level of their sins. If Allah wishes, they may be taken out of there and admitted into *Jannah.*

What to Expect in Jahannum

There are probably a few people out there thinking that they can get the best of both worlds. Why not enjoy this life to the max and then say '*La ilaha illallah*' at some point before you die and then you'll end up in *Jannah* after a short stint in Hellfire? How bad could it be? I'll tell you... And remember the horrors of Hell are even worse in reality than we can describe here!

> *...As often as their skins are roasted through, we shall change*
> *them for fresh skins, that they may taste the penalty...*
> (Surah An-Nisa 4:56)

If you wouldn't even put the tip of your finger in a flame for ten seconds, then why would you choose to go through that for any length of time?

And here's a taste of what is on the menu:

> *They will be given to drink from a boiling spring, no food*
> *will there be for them but a poisonous thorny plant,*
> *which will neither nourish nor avail against hunger.*
> (Surah Al-Ghashiyah 88:7)

The main purpose behind the description of Hellfire is not just to scare us but to ignite in our hearts the urge to take the actions needed to avoid that fire. When we are truly afraid of this, only then will we take the necessary steps to stay out of this danger that we have been warned about. 'Umar ibn Al-Khattab ﷺ said:

"Increase in your remembrance of the Fire, for its heat is extreme, its bottom is distant, and its whips are of iron." (Tirmidhi)

There wouldn't be a single criminal left on the face of this earth were people to remember the horror of *Jahannum*!

What to Expect in Jannah

We have spent a great deal of the book emphasising that our goal is *Jannah* and that should make up for all the sacrifice and suffering that we go through in this world. So what do we actually have to look forward to? Now again remember that we are too limited to understand and visualise the magnificence and sheer luxury of *Jannah*, but the following descriptions from the Qur'an and *hadith* should be enough to whet your appetite!

Enter Paradise, you and your wives, in happiness. Trays of gold and cups will be passed round them, (there will be) therein all that the inner-selves could desire, and all that the eyes could delight in, and you will abide therein forever. This is the Paradise which you have been made to inherit because of your deeds which you used to do (in the life of the world). Therein for you will be fruits in plenty, of which you will eat (as you desire). (Surah Az-Zukhruf 43:70-73)

But the greatest reward for us in *Jannah* will be to view the appearance of Allah. Despite having all that our hearts desire, the greatest reward for the inhabitants of *Jannah* will be to see Allah, the Mighty and Majestic. There will be nothing more delightful than looking at Him. Suhayb ibn Sinan ar-Rumi ﷺ narrated that the Messenger of Allah ﷺ said:

"When those deserving of Paradise enter Paradise, the Blessed and Exalted will ask: 'Do you wish Me to give you anything more?' They will say: 'Have You not brightened our faces? Have You not made us enter Paradise and saved us from Fire?' He (Allah) will then lift the veil (from their eyes), and of things given to them nothing will be dearer to them than the sight of their Lord, the Mighty and the Glorious." (Muslim)

When we see a really scenic place on earth, for example a beautiful valley surrounded by majestic mountains or a white beach with palm trees and clear turquoise water, our eyes wish to keep feasting on the gorgeous view and never have to look at anything drab again. Imagine how beautiful Allah must be that the greatest pleasure in *Jannah* will be the sight of Allah's Face.

There will be physical comforts beyond all imagination: palaces, jewels, gardens, exquisite food and refreshing drink. A person has only to desire these things and they will be made available to him. In fact, anything and everything that the heart desires is his. In addition to all these physical comforts, there will be complete contentment, peace of mind and tranquillity, states that we long for in this world will be ours in *Jannah* forever. We will not sorrow or grieve, regret or be stressed in any way – what a blissful state! Abu Sa'id al-Khudri ؓ narrated that the Prophet ﷺ said:

"Allah will say to the inhabitants of Paradise, 'O inhabitants of Paradise!' They will say, 'O our Lord, we present ourselves and are at Your pleasure, and goodness rests in Your hands.' Then He will say, 'Are you contented?' And they will say, 'And how should we not be contented, O Lord, when You have given to us that which You have given to no one else of Your creation?' Then He will say, 'Would you not like Me to give you something better than that?' And they will say, 'O Lord and what thing is better than that?' And He will say, 'I shall cause My favour to descend upon you and thereafter shall never be displeased with you.'" (Bukhari)

Chapter 6

Beyond

Congratulations on having got your degree! You hold one of the keys to your future and this key will, *insha'Allah*, open the doors to the job of your choice. This may also come with status, a good salary, company car and so on. With the disposable income you have you can buy a house and go on annual holidays and generally have a great time. While all of this is attainable and within reach now that you have a degree, that alone does not determine your success.

Of course you have to continue to work hard. Everything will not just fall into your lap. But this is a good time to work out what you mean by success. If it is about having a huge house with luxury cars on the drive and status, then you will work hard to achieve these even if it means getting up early in the morning, working late into the night, and sacrificing your leisure time to study for professional qualifications. So now is a good time to think about what you want in life. Close your eyes and imagine yourself in your old age. What would make you content and what would make you regret missed opportunities? Do you imagine a comfortable old age as having lots of money and a big house or lots of children and grandchildren around you? Do you want to have travelled the world? What do you want to be remembered for after you die: your dress sense, your bank balance, your job title, your house and cars, or your generosity, kindness, piety, honesty and nobility of character?

However you define success now, whether consciously or unconsciously, is how you will behave so that you can achieve your goals. We have been given definitions of success in the Qur'an and *hadith*:

The Day when neither wealth nor sons will be of any use – except for those who come to Allah with sound and flawless hearts. (Surah Ash-Shu'ara 26:88-89)

The Prophet ﷺ said,

"He is successful who has accepted Islam, who has been provided with sufficient for his wants and been made content by Allah with what He has given him." (Muslim)

These short quotes explain to us who really qualifies to be called successful. It's not about houses, cars, money and children. It is someone who has accepted Islam as their way of life, who has his needs fulfilled and regardless of their circumstances and the sizes of their bank balance, they are content and possess a thankful heart – a heart that is free from jealousy, anger, arrogance, showing off, deceit, grudges against others and is constantly engaged in the remembrance of Allah.

Most people spend most of their time and efforts in the pursuit of money. A number of sins such as theft, killing, breaking the ties of kinship and dishonesty have their root in money. But we must realise that money is actually of very little use to us:

What terrible companions are the dirham and dinar. They do not benefit you until they leave you. (Al-Hasan Al-Basri)

And if it causes us to behave in ways that are not befitting of a Muslim and diverts us from our remembrance of Allah, then it is actually bad for us.

Of course, we all like the best of this world as well but we must remember that our provision was pre-ordained for us long before we came into existence. We will get what we are destined to get and if we are given wealth, then it is not our own doing but a test for us to see how we earn it, how we utilise it and if we remember Allah in our time of comfort.

Insha'Allah, I hope that my words have been of some use to you during your time at university and that it gives you something to think about. There is a *du'a* that I particularly like and would like to leave you with because, despite being only a few words long, it covers all that we could possible want:

'Rabbana aatina fi'd dunya hasanatan wa fil akhirati hasanatan wa qina adhaban nar'

"O Lord, grant us good in this world and in the Hereafter and protect us from the torment of the Fire."

Glossary

akhirah	the Next World, the Afterlife, the Hereafter
Al-'Arsh	The Throne of Allah
Al-Kursi	The Footstool of Allah
Alhamdulillah	'Praise be to Allah'
Allahu Akbar	'Allah is the Greatest'
as-Sirat	the narrow bridge which spans the Fire of Hell and which must be crossed in order to enter *Jannah*
attar	natural alcohol-free perfume oil. Using this is a *Sunnah* of the Prophet Muhammad ﷺ.
ayah	literally 'a sign' but generally used to mean a verse of the Qur'an
Barzakh	life in the grave that spans the time between death in this world and resurrection on the Day of Judgement
deen	religion in the broadest sense, way of life
dhikr	remembrance or mention of Allah
dinar	a gold coin
dirham	a silver coin

dunya	this world, the physical universe, as opposed to the *akhirah*
fard	a religious duty or an obligatory action
ghusl	full ritual bath of the whole body
hadith	the reported sayings or actions or traditions of the Prophet Muhammad ﷺ
hafiz	someone who has memorised the Qur'an
Hajj	the annual pilgrimage to Makkah which is the fifth of the five pillars of Islam
halal	lawful or permitted according to Islamic Law
haram	forbidden or unlawful according to Islamic Law
hijab	the dress code for a Muslim woman which defines that nothing except her face and hands should be visible in public
'ilm	knowledge
ibadah	act of worship
Iblis	Satan, the Devil, *Shaytan*
iman	usually translated as belief or faith and often used to refer to the strength of conviction in a Muslim
insha'Allah	'Allah willing' or 'If it is Allah's will'
Islam	submission to the will of Allah
istanja	the method of cleaning one's private parts with water after using the toilet
Jannah	Paradise, Heaven, the Garden
Jahannum	Hellfire
jinn	invisible beings made of smokeless fire
Jumu'ah	the Day of Congregating or Friday. The *Jumu'ah* prayer refers to the prayer performed instead of *dhuhr* in congregation.

La ilaha illallah	'There is no god but Allah.' The first part of the declaration of faith.
masjid	mosque
mu'min	a believer, a person that has complete submission to the will of Allah, and has faith firmly established in his heart
Muslim	a follower of the religion of Islam; someone who submits to the will of Allah
Munkar and Nakir	the two angels who question the dead in their grave
nafl	voluntary acts of worship. One is rewarded for doing these but not punished for leaving them.
niyyah	intention
qadar	the Decree of Allah
qiblah	the direction faced towards in *salah*, towards the Ka'bah in Makkah
Qur'an	Allah's revelation to mankind through the Angel Jibril to the Prophet Muhammad ﷺ
rak'at	pl. of *rakah* which is one unit of *salah*
Ramadan	the ninth month of the Islamic calendar in which fasting is prescribed
riba	usury, gaining profit without effort
Sahabah	the Companions of the Prophet Muhammad ﷺ; those people that spoke with or met with the Prophet ﷺ at least once during his lifetime
salaam	the Muslim greeting of peace
salah	the ritual or prescribed five times daily prayer, which is the second pillar of Islam. These are *Fajr*, *Dhuhr*, *Asr*, *Maghrib* and *Isha*.

Shaytan	Satan, the Devil
SubhanAllah	'Glorified is Allah'
Sunnah	The practice of the Prophet Muhammad ﷺ
surah	pl. *suwar*; a chapter of the Qur'an
taqwa	the awe or fear of Allah that propels a person to do good and righteous actions and keep away from wrong actions
'ulama	scholars
wudu	ablution for ritual purification from minor impurities before performing *salah*
Zakah	wealth-tax payable on certain assets, the third pillar of Islam
zina	voluntary sexual intercourse between persons not married to each other
ﷺ	*sallallahu alayhi wa salaam* (may the peace and blessings of Allah be upon him). This is always said after the name of the Prophet Muhammad ﷺ.
ؓ	*radiallahu anhu* (may Allah be pleased with him). This is always said after the names of the Companions of the Prophet ﷺ.
ؓ	*radiallahu anha* (may Allah be pleased with her). This is always said after the names of the female Companions of the Prophet ﷺ.
ؑ	*alayhi salam* (peace be upon him). This is always said after the names of the prophets.

Glossary

Bibliography

Qur'an

The Holy Qur'an: Text, Translation and Commentary, Abdullah Yusuf Ali, Amana Corporation, 1989

The Meaning of the Glorious Qur'an, Muhammad Marmaduke Pickthall, Islamic Call Society, 1970

The Noble Qur'an: A New Rendering of its Meaning in English, Abdalhaqq and Aisha Bewley, Ta-Ha Publishers, 2011

Hadith

Riyad as-Saliheen, compiled by An-Nawawi, translated by Abdur Rehman Shad, Kazi Publications, Vol. 1, 1988

Riyad as-Saliheen, compiled by An-Nawawi, translated by Abdur Rehman Shad, Kazi Publications, Vol. 2, 1988

Daily Hadith iPhone Application by Adaptive Solutions Inc.

Seerah

The Life of Muhammad ﷺ, Tahia Al-Ismail, Ta-Ha Publishers, 2nd Edition, 2006

Other Books

A Concise Description of Jannah and Jahannum, Shaikh 'Abd al-Qadir Al-Jilani, translated by Muhtar Holland, Ta-Ha Publishers, 2010

Ad-Dunya: The Believer's Prison, The Disbelievers Paradise, Muhammad 'Abd ar-Rahman 'Iwad, translated by Asadullah Yates, Dar Al-Taqwa, 1997

After Death, Life!, Ruqaiyyah Waris Maqsood, Talha Publication, 2001

Dealing with Lust and Greed According to Islam, Sheikh 'Abd al-Hamid Kishk, Dar Al- Taqwa, 1995

Fortress of the Muslim, Compiled by Sa'id Wahf Al-Qahtani, Darussalam, 2006

Glimpses of Life After Death, Alpha Mahmoud Bah, Ta-Ha Publishers, 2001 [out of print]

Glossary of Islamic Terms, Aisha Bewley, Ta-Ha Publishers, 1998

Historic Judgement on Interest, Justice Maulana Muhammad Taqi Usmani, Darul Ishaat, 2000

In the Early Hours: Reflections on Spiritual and Self Development, Khurram Murad, Revival, 2000

Overcoming Trials and Tribulations, Ruqaiyah Abdullah, Ta-Ha Publishers, 2nd Edition, 2005

Patience and Gratitude, Ibn Qayyim al-Jawziyyah, translated by Nasiruddin al-Khattab, Ta-Ha Publishers, 1997

The Fresher's Guide, James Cormack and Luka Blackman-Gibbs, 2009

The Muslim Marriage Guide, Ruqaiyyah Waris Maqsood, Goodword Books, 1998

The Perfect Prayer, Dr Musharaf Hussain Al-Azhari, The Invitation Publishing House, 2001

The Remembrance of Death and the Afterlife, Al-Ghazali, translated by TJ Winter, Islamic Texts Society, 1989

Torch Bearers: Scholars of Islam iPhone Application by Ihsaan Fusion